UKRAINIAN PHRASEBOOK

JIM DINGLEY
OLENA BEKH

Ukrainian phrasebook
1st edition

Published by
Lonely Planet Publications
Head Office: PO Box 617, Hawthorn, Vic 3122, Australia
Branches: 155 Filbert St, Suite 251, Oakland, CA 94607, USA
10 Barley Mow Passage, Chiswick, W4 4PH, UK
71 bis rue du Cardinal Lemoine, 75005 Paris, France

Printed by
Colorcraft Ltd, Hong Kong

Cover Photograph
Playing chess, detail (George Wesely)

Published
August 1996

National Library of Australia Cataloguing in Publication Data

Bekh, Olena, 1962-
Ukrainian phrasebook.

1st ed.
Includes index.
ISBN 0 86442 339 X.

1. Ukrainian language - Conversation and phrase-books - English. I. Dingley, James, 1942-. II. Title. (Series: Lonely Planet language survival kit).

491.7983421

Contents

About the Authors

James Dingley is a senior lecturer in Ukrainian Studies at the University of London and he moonlights as the Vice-President of the International Association for Belarusian Studies. Jim is married with two daughters.

Olena Bekh is a post-doctoral fellow at the Institute of International Relations at the Taras Shevchenko University in Kyiv. She has a PhD in linguistics and has taught Ukrainian and Russian in Kyiv and London. Olena is married with one son.

From the Publisher

This book was written by Jim Dingley and Olena Bekh. It was edited by Louise Callan and proofread by Sally Steward. Penelope Richardson was responsible for the illustrations and design and Simon Bracken designed the cover. Thanks to Dan Levin for assistance with the Cyrillic script.

Introduction

Following the fall of the Soviet Union, Ukraine recovered its independence and began the process of rediscovering its history and culture. Its economic potential and strategic importance ensure that it has an important role to play on the world stage. Ukrainians refer to their country as 'Ukraine' rather than 'the Ukraine' as the latter implies that it is just a region, not an independent country. Ukrainian is the sole official language of the country and the first language of the majority of the population, but there are more reasons for learning some Ukrainian. Anyone visiting Ukraine now who shows even a slight familiarity with the language will be sure of a very warm welcome!

The language of Ukraine has had a turbulent evolution. The written form of Ukrainian was banned by the tsars in the 19th century. In the 1920s the Soviets allowed the language to thrive in schools and publications but Stalin's policy of 'Russification' meant that it was supplanted by Russian in the universities and little was allowed to be published in Ukrainian. Political factors were largely responsible for the development of what was regarded as 'proper' Ukrainian. The Ukrainian used in this book is the standard language spoken in the capital, Kyiv (Kiev), and other major centres.

Ukrainian belongs to the Slavonic group of the Indo-European family of languages, and is most closely related to Russian. It is spoken by about 50 million people in Ukraine and by considerable numbers in Poland, Slovakia, Romania and in Canada, the USA and Australia. The total number of speakers is probably around 60 million. Three main dialects are recognised: northern, south-western and south-eastern.

It uses the Cyrillic alphabet (so called after St Cyril who supposedly invented it in the ninth century to help spread Orthodox Christianity among the pagan Slavs). This alphabet is not as incomprehensible as it may appear at first. You will be able to recognise many words, eg музика is 'music', театр is theatre, автобус is 'bus'. Others, because of their common Indo-European origin, are related, but it takes a great leap of faith to believe that хліб ('bread') is the same in origin as the English 'loaf' or, even more fantastic, that верблюд ('camel') actually comes from the Greek word for 'elephant'!

By showing that you know some Ukrainian you are sharing in the adventure of freedom that the Ukrainian people themselves are now experiencing. We wish you good luck on your journey to Ukraine and the Ukrainian language. Бажаємо щасливої дороги! *(bazhayemo shchaslivoyee dorohi!)*

Abbreviations Used In This Book

adj	adjective
adv	adverb
f	feminine
inf	informal
m	masculine
n	noun
neut	neuter
pl	plural
pol	polite
prep	preposition
sg	singular
v	verb

Getting Started

The most common greeting in Ukrainian is Добридень *(do**bri**den')*. Try to memorise the small – but important – words like Так *(tak)* for 'Yes' and Ні *(nee)* for 'No'. You will hear Дякую. ***(dya**kooyoo)* for 'Thank you' and 'Please' is Будь ласка *(bood' **las**ka)* or Прошу *(**pro**shoo)*. When you are meeting people you'll find the phrases on page 34 useful and, if you want to join in the conversation, turn to page 46 for some handy conversation fillers. The phrases on page 47 will help if you are having trouble making yourself understood and in case of emergencies, turn to page 213.

Pronunciation

The Alphabet

Beware of the letters that look like English ones, but in fact stand for quite different sounds.

А	а	as in f**a**ther
Б	б	as in **b**ad
В	в	as in **v**ale or **w**ood
Г	г	as in **h**at, but with more voice
Ґ	ґ	as in **g**ood
Д	д	as in **d**og (try pronouncing it with the tongue behind your top teeth)
Е	е	as in **e**nd
Є	є	as in **ye**s
Ж	ж	'zh' as in plea**s**ure
З	з	as in **z**oo
И	и	as in b**i**t
І	і	as in b**ee**t
Ї	ї	as in **yea**st
Й	й	as in **y**et; always pronounced strongly, even at the end of a word)
К	к	as in **k**ick
Л	л	as in **l**and
М	м	as in **m**uch
Н	н	as in **n**o
О	о	as in **o**r, with rounded lips
П	п	as in **p**ot
Р	р	as in **r**ot (try rolling it)

С	с	as in **s**ad
Т	т	as in **t**op
У	у	as in t**oo**
Ф	ф	as in **f**un
Х	х	as the 'ch' in Scottish ***loch***
Ц	ц	as in Pa**ts**y
Ч	ч	as in **ch**at
Ш	ш	as in **sh**ot
Щ	щ	'shch' as in fre**sh ch**eese
Ю	ю	as in **you**th
Я	я	as in **ya**rd
Ь	ь	the 'soft sign'; it softens the consonant before it. The consonant is pronouned as if there were a short 'y' sound after it, eg compare the 'noo' sound in 'ca**noe**' with the 'nyoo' sound in 'si**new**'.

As you can see the letter ж becomes *zh* in the pronunciation guide. There are some words in Ukrainian where the two letters з (represented in the transliterations by *z*) and г (represented by *h*) come together, eg Згода! ('Agreed!'). If this word was transcribed as ***zhoda***, confusion could arise. Wherever the two letters зг come together in a word, they will appear in capital letters in the transliterations *(ZH)* so as not to confuse them with the sound of ж (as the 's' in 'pleasure').

Diphthongs

The diphthongs (vowel combinations) of Ukrainian consist of a vowel followed by the letter й):

ай	as in h**i**de
ей	as in w**ay**
ий	as in b**i**t followed by a strong 'y' sound
ій	as in b**ea**t followed by a strong 'y' sound
ой	as in b**oy**
уй	as in L**oui**s (without pronouncing the 's')

Transliteration

The transliteration system used in this book may not always correspond to those used in other books on Ukrainian. The formal systems used elsewhere, usually based on that employed by the Library of Congress, are intended to provide a uniform method of spelling Ukrainian words in the Roman script. Probably the greatest significant difference is in the transliteration of the letter и. We use 'i' as the closest equivalent sound in English, whereas other systems tend to use 'y', which is also the transliteration of й.

Since independence Ukrainians have become increasingly aware of the need to make the truly Ukrainian forms of city names internationally known. Ukraine's capital city is still widely known as Kiev – but this is the Russian form. By government decree of 14 October 1995 the name of the city is spelled Kyiv in Roman script. In our transliteration the city of Kyiv, Київ becomes ***ki**yeew*. Чернігів is another important Ukrainian city; it will be transliterated as 'Chernihiv' in English sentences (although it is perhaps more widely known as Chernigov), and as *cher**nee**heew* for pronunciation purposes. Ukraine's major port on the Black Sea is Одеса, ***O**desa*, rather than the Russian, *Odessa*.

You may also see a few Ukrainian words spelt with an apostrophe. This does not represent a sound. It means that the 'y' sound following it should be strongly pronounced.

A note on the letter В

As you can see from the list on page 10, this letter has two possible pronunciations, *v* and *w*. It has the *v* sound when it comes before a vowel, and *w* when it comes before a consonant or at the end of a word, eg Київ (the capital of Ukraine) is pronounced ***ki**yeew*; слово ('word') is pronounced ***slo**vo* but без слів ('without words') is pronounced *bez sleew*.

You will find that there are words which are sometimes spelt with в at the beginning, and at other times with у, eg 'at home', вдома / удома *(w**do**ma/oo**do**ma)*. If the previous word ends in a vowel, then в will be used; if it ends in a consonant, у will be used.

Stress

Stressed syllables are indicated by **bold** in the transliterations.

Intonation

This is much the same as in English. Intonation falls at the end of a sentence which is a statement but rises for a question.

Grammar

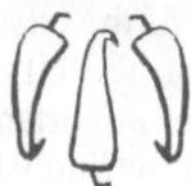

Sentence Structure

Word order is the same as in English (subject-verb-object). Sometimes the subject comes last to put special emphasis on it:

I live in London. *ya zhivoo wlondonee*	Я живу в Лондоні.
The President of Ukraine lives in this building. *oo ts'omoo boodinkoo zhive prezident ookrayeeni*	У цьому будинку живе президент України.

(lit: in this building lives President of Ukraine)

Articles

Ukrainian uses neither the definite article ('the') nor the indefinite article ('a'); so, дім *(deem)* can mean 'house', 'a house', 'the house', according to context.

Nouns

Gender

Nouns in Ukrainian can be masculine, feminine or neuter. Nouns that are masculine usually end in a 'hard' consonant, ie a consonant not followed by the 'soft sign' (ь) or by й – but there are exceptions:

GRAMMAR

boy	***khlopchik***	хлопчик
table	*steel*	стіл
exit	***vikheed***	вихід
tram	***tramvay***	трамвай
day	*den'*	день

Feminine nouns end in -a or -я or a soft consonant:

girl	***deewchina***	дівчина
book	***kniha***	книга
poetry	*poezeeya*	поезія
salt	*seel'*	сіль

Neuter nouns end in -o or -e and some end in -я making them appear feminine:

apple	***yablooko***	яблуко
sea	***more***	море
name	***eemya***	ім'я

Plurals

To make a noun plural in Ukrainian, add -и, -і or ї to the end. Feminine nouns drop the final -a of the singular form before adding the plural ending:

book	***kniha***	книга
books	***knihi***	книги

Neuter nouns change -o to -a and -e to -a or -я. Neuter nouns ending in -я generally do not change in the plural, except for:

name	***eemya***	ім'я
names	***imena***	імена

Some Ukrainian nouns in the singular correspond to an English plural:

biscuits	*pechivo*	печиво

and vice versa:

door	*dveree*	двері (pl - the word has no singular)

Cases

Ukrainian nouns change their endings according to their function in the sentence, ie whether they are the subject, object, indirect object, etc. No attempt is going to be made here to list all the cases and their endings, but the following notes on three main cases may help you sort out the structure of some of the phrases in this book. The ending of a noun helps to identify its case:

• **Nominative** – this is the dictionary form. A noun in the nominative case is the **subject** of a sentence:

The taxi driver works every day.		
	taksist pratsyooye shchodnya	Таксист працює щодня

• **Accusative** – a noun in the accusative case is the **object** of a sentence (on the 'receiving end' of a verb). Generally, masculine and neuter nouns have the same form as the nominative case. A feminine noun in the accusative changes the -a ending of its nominative form to -y in the singular. Generally, for plural it remains the same as the nominative case:

I want to buy **a car**.
ya khochoo koopiti mashinoo — Я хочу купити машину.
We love **Yalta.**
mi lyoobimo yaltoo — Ми любимо Ялту.

• **Dative** – a noun in the dative case is the **indirect object** of a sentence. In the sentence 'Give the money to me', 'money' is the direct object (ie, the accusative case) and 'me' is the indirect object (ie, the dative case). Sometimes the preposition 'for' is used in instances where Ukrainian uses the dative, eg 'I want to buy a present for my wife.' There will probably be little need to be concerned with the endings of nouns.

Pronouns

Personal Pronouns

	Singular		Plural	
1st person	I	я *(ya)*	we	ми *(mi)*
2nd person	you	ти *(ti)*	you	ви *(vi)*
3rd person	he	він *(veen)*	they	вони *(voni)*
	she	вона *(vona)*		
	it	воно *(vono)*		

The second person singular, ти *(ti),* is the familiar form of 'you'; and should only be used to someone you know well, unless you are invited to use it. Always address people with ви *(vi)*, which is also the polite singular form of 'you'. When used to refer to one person it is written with a capital letter.

Demonstrative Pronouns

The demonstrative pronouns in English are 'this', 'these', 'that', 'those'. The most useful demonstrative pronoun in Ukrainian is це *(tse)*, which means 'this/that is' or 'these/those are':

This is my passport. *tse meey **pas**port*	Це мій паспорт.
These are her suitcases. *tse yeeyee valeezi*	Це її валізи.

Possession

The following words, like adjectives (see page 19), change their form according to the gender and number of the noun they refer to:

my/mine	*meey/mo**ya**/moye/ moyee*	мій / моя / моє / мої (pl)
your/yours (inf)*	*tveey/tvo**ya**/ tvoye/tvoyee*	твій / твоя / твоє / твої (pl)
your/yours (pl, pol)	*vash/**va**sha/ **va**she/**va**shee*	ваш / ваша / ваше / ваші (pl)
our/ours	*nash/**na**sha/ **na**she/**na**shee*	наш / наша / наше / наші (pl)
his	*yo**ho***	його
her/hers	*yee**yee***	її
their/theirs	*yeekh*	їх

* Use твій only in situations when you would use the polite personal pronoun ти.

GRAMMAR

Adjectives

Adjectives in Ukrainian change their form according to the gender and number of the noun they refer to. Adjectives are listed in dictionaries in the masculine nominative singular form. The ending is -ий or -ій. This ending changes to -а or -я for feminine nouns, and to -е or -є for neuter nouns. The plural ending for both masculine and feminine nouns is -і or -ї.

beautiful	***har**niy*	гарний

beautiful building (m)
***har**niy boo**di**nok* — гарний будинок

beautiful girl (f)
***har**na **deew**china* — гарна дівчина

beautiful city (neut)
***har**ne **mee**sto* — гарне місто

beautiful buildings (m, pl)
***har**nee boo**din**ki* — гарні будинки

Adverbs

Adverbs in Ukrainian are formed by changing the ending of the corresponding adjective in the masculine nominative singular: -ий changes to -о or -е. Adverbs usually come second in a Ukrainian sentence. добрий *(dobriy)*, meaning 'good', changes to добре *(dobre)* to become the adverb 'well':

a good man	***dob**riy cholo**veek***	добрий чоловік

He speaks Ukrainian well.
*veen **dob**re rozmow**lya**ye ookray**eens**'koyoo **mo**voyoo* — Він добре розмовляє українською мовою.

Here are a few commonly used adverbs:

wonderful (adj)	*choo**do**viy*	чудовий
Wonderful! (adv)	*choo**do**vo!*	чудово!
good/kind (adj)	***do**briy*	добрий
Good/Fine! (adv)	***do**bre*	Добре!
cold (adj)	*kho**lo**dniy*	холодний
It's cold. (adv)	***kho**lodno*	Холодно.

Verbs

The ending of a verb tells us who the subject is as well as the tense of the verb (present, past or future). The dictionary form of a verb is called an infinitive. In English infinitives are indicated by the word 'to': 'to see', 'to write', etc. In Ukrainian the infinitive form ends in -ти. Most Ukrainian verbs actually have two infinitive forms.

GRAMMAR

Present

An infinitive which has the letter a before the ending -ти, usually takes the following endings in the present tense:

to read	*chi**ta**ti*	читати
I read	*ya chi**ta**yoo*	я читаю
you read (inf)	*ti chi**ta**yesh*	ти читаєш
he/she reads	*veen/vo**na** chi**ta**ye*	він / вона читає
we read	*mi chi**ta**yemo*	ми читаємо
you read	*vi chi**ta**yete*	ви читаєте
they read	*vo**ni** chi**ta**yoot'*	вони читають

With и before the infinitive ending, the verb will usually take these endings in the present tense:

to see	*bachiti*	бачити
I see	*ya ba**choo***	я бачу
you see (inf)	*ti **ba**chish*	ти бачиш
he/she sees	*veen/vo**na** ba**chit'***	він / вона бачить
we see	*mi ba**chi**mo*	ми бачимо
you see	*vi **ba**chite*	ви бачите
they see	*vo**ni** ba**chat'***	вони бачать

As usual, there are a few exceptions so don't worry if you come across some verbs which do not correspond to these patterns.

Past

To form the past tense, drop the ending -ти from the infinitive of the verb and add -в for a masculine singular subject; -ла for a feminine singular subject and -ло for a neuter singular subject. If the subject is plural the ending is -ли for all genders.

I (m) saw the university. *ya **ba**chiw ooneever**si**tet*	Я бачив університет.
I (f) saw the church. *ya **ba**chila **tser**kvoo*	Я бачила церкву.
We saw a good restaurant. *mi **ba**chili **do**briy resto**ran***	Ми бачили добрий ресторан.

Future

As a general rule, use the present tense endings. Ukrainian verbs do have future tense endings but you will be understood if you just use the rules for the present tense. You could also use words that refer to the future, eg 'tomorrow', завтра ***(zawtra)***, and 'next week', наступного тижня ***(nastoopnoho tizhnya)***. See also 'To Be' below.

Negatives

To make a sentence negative, put не *(ne)* in front of the verb:

I don't know.
*ya ne **zna**yoo* — Я не знаю.

GRAMMAR

To Be

There is no word in Ukrainian corresponding to the English 'am', 'is', 'are'. It is understood from the sentence.

I am from Australia.
*ya z aw**stra**leeyee* — Я з Австралії.
(lit: I from Australia)

This is an interesting museum.
*tse tsee**ka**viy moo**zey*** — Це цікавий музей.
(lit: this interesting museum)

You can use the word є to mean 'am', 'are' or 'is', but it is not essential. It is often used to mean 'there is/there are':

There is a good restaurant in Poltava.
*oo pol**ta**vee ye **dob**riy resto**ran*** — У Полтаві є добрий ресторан.
(lit: in Poltava there is good restaurant)

The negative form 'there is/are not' is немає *(nemaye)*:

There's no restaurant here.
toot nemaye restoranoo Тут немає ресторану.
(lit: here there is no restaurant)

To Have

There are two ways of saying 'to have'; both are in regular use. The first way is simply to use the infinitive form of 'to have' – мати *(mati)*. It takes the same endings as the verb 'to read' (читати) – see page 20:

I have a visa.
ya mayoo veezoo Я маю візу.

The second way is a little more complex. You use the preposition в or у ('to'), followed by a form of the verb 'to be':

I have a visa.
oo mene ye veeza В мене немае візи.
(lit: to me there is a visa)
We have ...
oo nas ye ... У нас є ...

Modals

Modal verbs express an ability, necessity, desire or need. In English they are 'can', 'may', 'must', 'should', 'want', 'need'.

Can

Can you read?
chi ti mozhesh chitati? Чи ти можеш читати?

GRAMMAR

He can eat and drink a lot.
*veen **mo**zhe **yee**sti y **pi**ti ba**ha**to* — Він може їсти й пити багато.

When 'can' means 'may/have permission', Ukrainian uses just one word можна ***(mozhna)***, regardless of the subject:

May I take photographs here?
***mozh**na (me**nee**) toot fotohrafoo**va**ti?* — Можна (мені) тут фотографувати?

Yes, you may.
*tak, **mozh**na* — Так, можна.

No, you may not.
*nee, ne**mozh**na* — Ні, неможна.

Must/Have To

The easiest way to say that you have to do something is to translate the English expression word for word into Ukrainian: 'have', мати ***(mati)***, followed by an infinitive:

I have to go.
*ya **ma**yoo **y**ti* — Я маю йти.

The word треба ***(treba)*** is also used to mean 'must/have to' but is used with a different form of the personal pronoun:

I must ...
***me**nee **tre**ba ...* — Мені треба …

Do you have to ...?
*vam **tre**ba ... ?* — Вам треба …?

Should/Ought To

The Ukrainian equivalent is повинен (m), повинна (f) and повинні (pl), *(povinen, povinna, povinnee)*.

You (pl) ought to know where the museum is.	
vi povinnee znati, de moozey	Ви повинні знати, де музей.

Want/Would like

The infinitive is хотіти *(khoteeti)*:

I want ...	
*ya **kho**choo*	Я хочу …
What do you want?	
*shcho vi **kho**chete*	Що ви хочете?
I would like to buy ...	
ya khoteew bi/khoteela b koopiti ...	Я хотів би (m)/хотіла б (f) купити …
Would you like ...?	
vi khoteeli b...?	Ви хотіли б …?

Need

The Ukrainian word is потрібен (m), потрібна (f) or потрібні (pl), *(potreeben, potreebna, potreebnee)*. The form of this verb depends upon what is needed, not on who does the needing, that is, the form of the verb depends on the object, not the subject:

I need a dictionary.	
menee potreeben slownik	Мені потрібен словник.
(lit: to me a dictionary is necessary)	

GRAMMAR

Do you need help?
*vam po**treeb**na do**po**mo**ha?*** Вам потрібна допомога?
(lit: to you needed help?)

Reflexive Verbs
The words 'myself', 'himself', etc (as in 'I am washing myself', 'He can see himself in the mirror') are called reflexive pronouns. There is an affix in Ukrainian – ся *(sya)* – which is added to the verb to indicate a reflexive. Some verbs are reflexive in Ukrainian that are not reflexive in English, eg сміятися *(smee**ya**tisya)*, 'to laugh'.

GRAMMAR

Prepositions

Ukrainian prepositions are tied up very closely with the case system of nouns, and this makes them complicated to use. However, you will be understood if you combine the following prepositions with the nominative (or dictionary) form of the noun. Some prepositions have different meanings, according to the case of the noun:

to	*oo/w/do*	у / в / до
in	*oo/w*	у / в
on	*na*	на
from	*z/veed*	з / від
with	*z*	з
without	*bez*	без
through/via/in (time)	***che**rez*	через
at (time)	*o*	о

Questions

Just using intonation is enough to form a question. You can also precede your question with the little word чи? *(chi?)* or follow it with так? *(tak?)* . These are the equivalent of the English tag questions 'isn't it?', 'aren't you?', 'don't they?', etc

Do you live in London?
vi zhivete wlondonee, tak? Ви живете в Лондоні, так?
(lit: you live in London, don't you?)

Question Words

who?	*khto?*	хто?
what?	*shcho?*	що?
why?	*chomoo?*	чому?
when?	*koli?*	коли?

Ukrainian makes a clear distinction with 'where':

where?	*de?*	де?
(to) where?	*koodi?*	куди?

Where do you live
de vi zhivete? Де ви живете?
Where are you going?
koodi vi ydete? Куди ви йдете?

GRAMMAR

GRAMMAR

Conjunctions

and*	*ee/y/ta*	і / й / та
but	*ale*	але
because	*tomoo shcho*	тому що
therefore	*tomoo*	тому
if	*yakshcho*	якщо

* The form used depends on the surrounding sounds – it's always safe to use i.

Some Useful Words

someone	*khtos'*	хтось
no-one	*neekoho*	нікого
something	*shchos'*	щось
nothing	*neechoho*	нічого
somewhere	*des'*	десь
nowhere	*neede*	ніде
here	*toot*	тут
there	*tam*	там
Here is ...	*os'* ...	Ось ...
There is ...	*on* ...	Он ...
Yes.	*tak*	Так.
No.	*nee*	Ні.
Maybe.	*maboot'*	Мабуть.

Greetings & Civilities

Greetings

The neutral greeting in Ukrainian is Добридень *(dobriden')*, rather like English 'Good day'. It can be used at any time of the day. Greetings more closely connected to a particular time of day include:

Good morning.
dobroho rankoo
доброго ранку.

Good afternoon.
***dobriy** den'*
добрий день.

Good evening.
dobriy vecheer
добрий вечір.

Hello/Good day. ***dobriden'*** Добридень.
(general greeting)

Use these informal expressions only if you are on friendly terms with the person to whom you are speaking:

Hi!	*pri**veet**!*	Привіт!
How are things?	*yak **spra**vi?*	Як справи?
How's life?	*yak zhi**ttya**?*	Як життя?
What's new?	*ya**kee** no**vi**ni?*	Які новини?
	*shcho w**te**be no**vo**ho?*	Що в тебе нового?
Fine, thanks.	***do**bre, **dya**kooyoo*	Добре, дякую.
Great.	*choo**do**vo*	Чудово.
OK.	*nor**mal'**no*	Нормально.
Not bad.	*nepo**ha**no*	Непогано.
Nothing new.	*nee**cho**ho no**vo**ho ne**ma**ye*	Нічого нового немає.
And you?	*a oo vas?*	А у вас?
	*a w **te**be?*	А в тебе? (inf)

Goodbyes

Goodbye.	*dopo**ba**chennya*	До побачення.
	*do**zoo**streechee* (lit: to our next meeting)	До зустрічі.
Good night.	*dob**ra**neech*	Добраніч.

More informal goodbyes include:

Cheerio!	*shchas**li**vo*	Щасливо!
Bye!	*boo**vay**/ boo**vay**te pa!*	Бувай (sg)/ бувайте (pl) па!

It was very nice meeting you.
boolo doozhe priyemno poznayomitisya z vami — Було дуже приємно познайомитися з вами.

I hope we shall see other again soon.
spodeevayoosya, shcho mi nezabarom shche raz pobachimosya — Сподіваюся, що ми незабаром ще раз побачимося.

I'm sorry, but I must be going.
pereproshooyoo, ale ya wzhe mayoo yti — перепрошую, але я вже маю йти.

Please give my regards to your husband/your wife.
bood' laska, peredayte priveet vashomoo choloveekovee/vasheey droozhinee — Будь ласка, передайте привіт вашому чоловікові / вашій дружині.

Attracting Someone's Attention

If you want to attract someone's attention in order to ask a question you should say Скажіть, будь ласка *(skazheet', bood' laska)* which means 'Tell me, please ...'. If you wish to enter someone's room or ask permission to do something, you should ask Можна? *(mozhna?)* which means 'May I?'

Civilities

Please.
bood' laska — Будь ласка.

Thank you (very much).
(doozhe) dyakooyoo — (Дуже) дякую.

Thanks for everything.
dyakooyoo za wse — Дякую за все.
Don't mention it.
proshoo — прошу.

Apologies

Excuse me.
vibachte (menee) — вибачте (мені).
probachte (menee) — пробачте (мені).
I'm (very) sorry.
(doozhe) pereproshooyoo — (Дуже) перепрошую.
Excuse me. (when squeezing through a crowd)
bood' laska, dozvol'te proyti — Будь ласка, дозвольте пройти.
It's OK/Never mind.
neechoho — Нічого.
Don't worry.
ne toorbooytesya — Не турбуйтеся.

Small Talk

You will find it easy to meet and talk with locals. Ukrainians enjoy lively conversation, especially with foreigners.

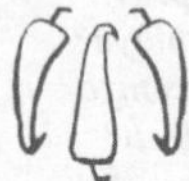

Top 10 Useful Phrases

These are the phrases that you will need most frequently:

Yes.	*tak*	Так.
No.	*nee*	Ні.
Please.	*bood' **las**ka/*	Будь ласка /
	***pro**shoo*	Прошу.
Thank you.	***dya**kooyoo*	Дякую.
Hello!	*dob**ri**den'!*	Добридень!
	*pri**veet**!*	Привіт! (inf)
How are you?	*yak **spra**vi*	Як справи? (inf)
Pleased to meet you.	***doo**zhe pri**yem**no*	Дуже приємно.
Excuse me.	*pere**pro**shooyoo*	Перепрошую.
Sorry.	***vi**bachte*	Вибачте.
Where is ...?	*de ...?*	Де ...?

It doesn't matter/It's all right.

*nee**cho**ho/oose ha**razd**/*	Нічого / Усе гаразд /
*ne khvi**lyoo**ytesya*	Не хвилюйтеся!

Friendly Chat

There is no straightforward way of asking a Ukrainian how they are. Here are some informal ways of asking 'How are you?'; try them out only on people you have come to know fairly well.

How are things?	*yak **spra**vi?*	Як справи?
How's life?	*yak zhit**tya**?*	Як життя?
How's the family?	*yak see**mya**?*	Як сім'я?
How are the kids?	*yak **dee**ti?*	Як діти?

Here are some possible replies:

Great!	*choo**do**vo*	Чудово.
Fine!	***do**bre*	Добре.
OK!	*nor**mal'**no*	Нормально.
Rotten!	*po**ha**no*	Погано.

Things couldn't be better!
***kra**shche ne boo**va**ye* Краще не буває.

Things can't get worse!
***heer**she **nee**koodi* Гірше нікуди.

Meeting People

In formal situations, shake hands when being introduced or introducing yourself. Women may have their hands kissed. Address someone by their first name and patronymic (a name derived from the first name of their father). The Ukrainian word for 'Mr', пан *(pan)*, changes to пане ***(pa**ne)* when you are addressing someone. There is no word for 'Miss' or 'Ms' but you can use the word пані ***(pa**nee)* which is also used to mean 'Mrs'.

Hello, Mr Krawchenko.
*dobriden', **pane** **krawchenko***
Добридень, пане Кравченко.

What is your name?
*yak vas zvoot'/yak vashe **eemya**?*
Як Вас звуть / Як Ваше ім'я?

My name is …
***mene** zvoot'...*
Мене звуть …
*moye **eemya** ...*
Моє ім'я …

Here is my business card.
*os' **moya** veezitna **kartka***
Їсь моя візитна картка.

Pleased to meet you.
*doozhe **priyemno***
Дуже приємно.

I'd like to introduce you to my ..	*poznay**om**tesya, tse meey ...*	Познайомтеся, це мій …
friend	*drooh*	друг
husband	*cholo**veek***	чоловік
colleague	*ko**le**ha*	колега
girlfriend	*mo**ya** **pod**rooha*	моя подруга
wife	*mo**ya** droo**zhi**na*	моя дружина

Nationalities

Where are you from?
zveedki vi? Звідки Ви?

I am from ...	*yaz ...*	Я з …
Australia	*aw**stra**leeyee*	Австралії
Canada	*ka**na**di*	Канади
China	*ki**ta**yoo*	Китаю
England	***an**hleeyee*	Англії
France	***fran**tseeyee*	Франції
Germany	*nee**mech**chini*	Німеччини
Ireland	*eer**lan**deeyee*	Ірландії
Italy	*ee**ta**leeyee*	Італії
Japan	*ya**po**neeyee*	Японії
the Middle East	*se**red**n'oho **skho**doo*	Середнього Сходу
New Zealand	*no**vo**yee ze**lan**deeyee*	Нової Зеландії
Scandinavia	*skandi**na**veeyee*	Скандинавії
Scotland	*shot**lan**deeyee*	Шотландії
South Africa	*peew**den**noyee **a**friki*	Південної Африки
Spain	*ee**spa**neeyee*	Іспанії
US		
Wales	*ooel'soo*	Уельсу

Age

How old are you?
***skeel'ki** vam ro**keew**?* — Скільки Вам років?

How old is your child?
***skeel'ki** ro**keew** va**sheey** di**tinee**?* — Скільки років Вашій дитині?

I am 24.
*me**nee** **dvatsyat'** cho**tiri** (**ro**ki)* — Мені 24 (роки).

He/She is 10.
*yo**moo**/**yeey** **desyat'** (ro**keew**)* — Йому (m)/їй (f) 10 (років).

(See Numbers & Amounts, page 165, for a full list of numbers.)

Occupations

What is your occupation?
*kim vi **pratsyoo**yete?* — Ким Ви працюєте?

In the following list the masculine form appears first, the feminine second.

I am a/an ...	*ya ...*	Я ...
accountant	*boo**hal**ter*	бухгалтер
actor	***ak**tor*	актор
	*ak**tri**sa*	актриса
architect	*arkhee**tek**tor*	архітектор
artist	*khoo**dozh**nik*	художник
	*khoo**dozh**nitsya*	художниця
businessperson	*beeznes**men***	бізнесмен (m)
	*dee**lo**va zheen**ka***	ділова жінка (f)
carpenter	*tes**lyar***	тесляр

SMALL TALK

chef	***koo**khar*	кухар
diplomat	*diplo**mat***	дипломат
doctor	***lee**kar*	лікар
	***lee**karka*	лікарка
driver	*vo**deey***	водій
engineer	*eenzhe**ner***	інженер
farmer	***fer**mer*	фермер
journalist	*zhoorna**leest***	журналіст
	*zhoorna**leest**ka*	журналістка
labourer	*robeet**nik***	робітник
	*robeet**nit**sya*	робітниця
lawyer	*yoo**rist***	юрист
musician	*moozi**kant***	музикант
nurse	*med**brat***	медбрат
	*medses**tra***	медсестра
office worker	*pratseew**nik***	працівник
	***o**feesoo*	офісу
	*pratseew**nit**sya*	працівниця
policeman/ policewoman	*polee**tsey**skiy*	поліцейський
politician	*po**lee**tik*	політик
postman	*listo**no**sha*	листоноша
priest	*svya**shchen**nik*	священник
research student	*aspee**rant***	аспірант
	*aspee**rant**ka*	аспірантка
sailor	*mo**ryak***	моряк
salesperson	*proda**vets**'*	продавець
scientist	*naoo**ko**vets'*	науковець
secretary	*sekre**tar***	секретар
	*sekre**tar**ka*	секретарка
soldier	*veeys'**ko**viy*	військовий

student	*stoo**dent***	студент
	*stoo**dent**ka*	студентка
teacher	*vikla**dach***	викладач
	*vikla**dach**ka*	викладачка
translator/ interpreter	*perekla**dach***	перекладач
	*perekla**dach**ka*	перекладачка
waiter	*ofeetsee**ant***	офіціант
	*ofeetsee**ant**ka*	офіціантка
writer	*pis'**men**nik*	письменник
	*pis'**men**nitsya*	письменниця

Where do you work?
*de vi pra**tsyoo**yete?* Де Ви працюєте?

I work in a/an/the ...	*ya pra**tsyoo**yoo w ...*	Я працюю в …
bank	***ban**koo*	банку
company '...'	*kom**pa**neeyee '...'*	компанії '…'
embassy	*po**sol'**stvee/*	посольстві /
	*amba**sa**dee*	амбасаді
hospital	*lee**kar**nee*	лікарні
newspaper	*ha**ze**tee*	газеті
restaurant	*resto**ra**nee*	ресторані
theatre	*te**a**tree*	театрі
university	*ooneeversi**te**tee*	університеті

I work in a ...	*ya pra**tsyoo**yoo na ...*	Я працюю на …
factory	*za**vo**dee/**fa**britsee*	заводі / фабриці
post office	***posh**tee*	пошті

Where do you study?
*de vi naw**cha**yetesya?* Де ви навчаєтеся?

I am studying in/at (a/an/the) ...	*ya naw**cha**yoosya w ...*	Я навчаюся в …
academy	*aka**de**meeyee*	академії
conservatoire	*konserva**to**reeyee*	консерваторії
institute	*eensti**too**tee*	інституті
school	***shko**lee*	школі
university	*ooneeversi**te**tee*	університеті

I am a postgraduate.
*ya naw**cha**yoosya w aspeeran**too**ree* — Я навчаюся в аспірантурі.

amateur	*a**ma**tor*	аматор
job (work)	*ro**bo**ta*	робота
job (position)	*po**sa**da*	посада
retired	*penseeo**ner***	пенсіонер (m)
	*penseeo**ner**ka*	пенсіонерка (f)
salary	*zaro**beet**na plat**nya***	заробітна платня
unemployed	*bezro**beet**niy*	безробітний (m)
	*bezro**beet**na*	безробітнйа (f)

Family

Are you married?
*vi od**roo**zheniy?* (to a man) — Ви одружений?
*za**meezh**nya?* (to a woman) — Заміжня?

I am (not) married.
*ya (ne) od**roo**zheniy* — Я (не) одружений. (m)
*ya (ne) za**meezh**nya* — Я (не) заміжня. (f)

Do you have a big family?
*oo vas velika seem**ya**?* — У вас велика сім'я?

Yes, I do.
*tak, ve**li**ka* — Так, велика.

No, not very.
*nee, ne **doo**zhe* — Ні, не дуже.

Do you have any children?
*oo vas ye **dee**ti?* — У вас є діти?

I don't have any children.
*oo **me**ne ne**ma**ye dee**tey*** — У мене немає дітей.

Do you have a son/daughter?
*vi **ma**yete **si**na/**don'**koo?* — Ви маєте сина/доньку?

I have a son and a daughter.
*ya **ma**yoo **si**na y **don'**koo.* — Я маю сина й доньку.

My daughter is younger.
***don'**ka mo**lod**sha* — донька молодша.

How many brothers/sisters do you have?
***skeel'**ki oo vas bra**teew**/ ses**ter**?* — Скільки у Вас братів/сестер?

I have one brother/two sisters.
*oo **me**ne o**din** brat/dvee **ses**tri* — У мене один брат/дві сестри.

Family Members

husband	*cholo**veek***	чоловік
wife	*droo**zhi**na*	дружина
mother	***ma**ti/**ma**ma*	мати/мама
father	***bat'**ko/**ta**to*	батько/тато
son	*sin*	син
daughter	***don'**ka*	донька
brother	*brat*	брат
sister	*ses**tra***	сестра
uncle	***dyad'**ko*	дядько
aunt	***teet**ka*	тітка
grandfather	*dee**doos'***	дідусь
grandmother	*ba**boo**sya*	бабуся
grandson	*o**nook***	онук
granddaughter	*o**nooch**ka*	онучка
old	***sta**riy*	старий
young	*molo**diy***	молодий
elder	***star**shiy*	старший
younger	*mo**lod**shiy*	молодший

Religion

What is your religion?

do yakoyee releeheeyee vi nalezhite? — До якої релігії ви належите?

(lit: to what religion do you belong?)

In the following list, the masculine form of the word appears first.

I am ...	ya ...	Я …
Buddhist	***buddist***	буддист
	buddistka	буддистка
Christian	*khristi**yan**in*	християнин
	*khristi**yan**ka*	християнка
Orthodox	*pravo**slaw**niy*	православний
	*pravo**slaw**na*	православна
Greek Catholic	*hrekoka**to**lik*	греко-католик
	*hrekokato**lich**ka*	греко-католичка
Roman Catholic	*rimoka**to**lik*	римо-католик
	*rimokato**lich**ka*	римо-католичка
Hindu	*eendoo**yeest***	індуїст
	*eendoo**yeest**ka*	індуїстка
Jewish	*eeoo**dey***	іудей
	*eeoo**dey**ka*	іудейка
Muslim	*moosool'**man**in*	мусульманин
	*moosool'**man**ka*	мусульманка

Expressing Likes & Dislikes

Do you like ...?

vam podobayet'sya ...? — Вам подобається …?

I like ... very much.	*menee doozhe podobayet'sya ...*	Мені дуже подобається ...
your country	*vasha krayeena*	ваша країна
the journey	*podorozh*	подорож
him/her/this	*veen/vona/tse*	він / вона / це
I (don't) like ...	*menee (ne) podobayet'sya ...*	Мені (не) подобається ...
the theatre	*teatr*	театр
reading books	*chitati knihi*	читати книги
playing sport	*zaymatisya sportom*	займатися спортом
singing	*speevati*	співати
playing the piano	*hrati na fortepyano*	грати на фортеп'яно
I (don't) like ...	*ya (ne) lyooblyoo ...*	Я (не) люблю ...
humour	*hoomor*	гумор
the summer	*leeto*	літо
travelling	*podorozhoovati*	подорожувати
the cinema	*keeno*	кіно

Expressing Feelings

Are you .../Do you feel ...?
vam ...? Вам ...?

I am/feel ...	*menee ...*	Мені ...
ashamed	*soromno*	соромно
bored	*noodno*	нудно
cold	*kholodno*	холодно
happy	*veselo*	весело
hot	*zharko*	жарко

sad	***soom**no*	сумно
sorry	*shko**da***	шкода
uncomfortable	*ne**zroo**chno*	незручно
warm	***tep**lo*	тепло

I'm in a hurry.
*ya pospee**sha**yoo* — Я поспішаю.

I'm hungry.
*ya **kho**choo **yee**sti* — Я хочу їсти.
(lit: I want to eat)

I'm thirsty.
*ya **kho**choo **pi**ti* — Я хочу пити.
(lit: I want to drink)

I feel sleepy.
*ya **kho**choo **spa**ti* — Я хочу спати.

I want to have a rest.
*ya **kho**choo veedpo**chi**ti* — Я хочу відпочити.

Expressing Opinions

I think ...	*ya **doo**mayoo ...*	Я думаю ...
I consider ...	*ya wva**zha**yoo ...*	Я вважаю ...
In my opinion ...	*na mo**yoo** **doom**koo ...*	На мою думку ...
Yes, (it is).	*tak, (**pra**vil'no)*	Так, (правильно).
No, (it isn't).	*nee, (ne **pra**vil'no)*	Ні, (не правильно).
I (dis)agree.	*ya (ne) **ZHo**den* *ya (ne) **ZHod**na*	Я (не) згоден. (m) Я (не) згодна. (f)

I'm not against it.
*ya ne **pro**ti* — Я не проти.

Making Conversation

Is that correct?	***pra**vil'no?*	Правильно?
You're right.	*vi **ma**yete **rat**seeyoo*	Ви маєте рацію.
Is that true?	*(tse) **praw**da?*	(Це) правда?
We'll see.	*po**ba**chimo*	Побачимо.
God knows!	***khto**zna!*	Хтозна!
Agreed!	***ZHo**da!*	Згода!
Great!	***ha**razd!*	Гаразд!
Of course!	*zvi**chay**no!*	Звичайно!
Without doubt!	*bezpe**rech**no!*	Безперечно!
No problem!	*ne**ma**ye prob**lem**!*	Немає проблем!
You don't have to!	*ne **tre**ba!*	Не треба!
It can't be!	*ne **mo**zhe **boo**ti!*	Не може бути!
I'm joking.	*ya zhar**too**yoo*	Я жартую.

You can't joke about that!
*ya**kee** **mo**zhoot' **boo**ti **zhar**ti* — Які можуть бути жарти!

You mustn't do that!
*ts'oho ne **mozhna** robiti* — Цього не можна робити!

That's impossible!
*tse nemozh**li**vo* — Це неможливо!

That's right/true!
***praw**da* — Правда!

That's not right/true!
*ne**praw**da* — Неправда!

You're mistaken.
*vi pomil**ya**yetesya* — Ви помиляєтеся.

That's going too far!
*tse za**nad**to* — Це занадто!

I wouldn't have said that.
*ya b tak ne ska**zaw**/ ska**za**la* — Я б так не сказав (m)/ сказала (f).

With great pleasure!
*z ve**li**kim zado**vo**lennyam!* — З великим задоволенням!

Language Difficulties

I'm a foreigner.
*ya eeno**ze**mets'* — Я іноземець. (m)
*ya eeno**zem**ka* — Я іноземка. (f)

I understand.
*ya rozoo**mee**yoo* — Я розумію.

I don't understand (you).
*ya (vas) ne rozoo**mee**yoo* — Я (Вас) не розумію.

I didn't understand what you said.
*ya ne zrozoo**meew**/ zrozoo**mee**la, shcho vi ska**za**li* — Я не зрозумів (m)/ зрозуміла (f), що ви сказали.

I'm sorry, what did you say?
*pere**pro**shooyoo, shcho vi ska**za**li?* — Перепрошую, що ви сказали?

I (don't) know ...	*ya (ne) **zna**yoo ...*	Я (не) знаю ...
how to say this	*yak tse ska**za**ti*	як це сказати
what this is called	*yak tse nazi**va**yet'sya*	як це називається

I don't speak Ukrainian very well yet.
*ya shche ne **doo**zhe **do**bre rozmow**lya**yoo ookra**yeen**s'koyoo **mo**voyoo* — Я ще не дуже добре розмовляю українською мовою.

I speak ...	*ya rozmow**lya**yoo ...*	Я розмовляю ...
Do you speak ...	*vi rozmow**lya**yete ... (**mo**voyoo)?*	Ви розмовляєте ... (мовою)?
English	*an**hleeys**'koyoo*	англійською
German	*nee**mets'**koyoo*	німецькою
French	*fran**tsooz'**koyoo*	французькою
Spanish	*ees**pans**'koyoo*	іспанською

What does this mean?
*shcho tse ozna**cha**ye?* — Що це означає?
What does ... mean?
*shcho ozna**cha**ye ...?* — Що означає ...?

Could you please ...?	*vi ne moh**lib** ...?*	Ви не моглиб ...?
speak slowly	*hovo**ri**ti po**veel'**no*	говорити повільно

repeat the question	*powtoriti zapitannya*	повторити запитання
repeat the last word	*powtoriti ostannye slovo*	повторити останнє слово

Useful Questions

Who is/are ...?	*khto ...?*	Хто ...?
this	*tse*	це
you	*vi*	Ви
these people	*tsee lyoodi*	ці люди
this man	*tsey choloveek*	цей чоловік
this woman	*tsya zheenka*	ця жінка
there	*tam*	там
last (in a queue)	*ostanniy*	останній

What ...?	*shcho ...?*	Що ...?
is this	*tse*	це
am I to do	*menee robiti*	мені робити
do you want	*vam potreebno*	Вам потрібно
happened	*trapilosya*	трапилося

What is this called?
yak tse nazivayet'sya? Як це називається?

USEFUL TIP

To turn a sentence into a question, just use the intonation of your voice OR tack the word так? (*tak?*) onto the end of the sentence.

Refer to page 27

Where is/are ...?	*de ...?*	Де ...?
the exit	*toot **vi**kheed*	тут вихід
my things	*moyee **re**chee*	мої речі
this situated	*tse zna**kho**dit'sya*	це знаходиться
Where ...?	*koo**di** ...?*	Куди ...?
do I have to go	***me**nee **tre**ba **y**ti*	мені треба йти
are we going	*mi yde**mo***	ми йдемо

How long are we going to have to wait?
*skeel'ki mi **boo**demo che**ka**ti?* — Скільки ми будемо чекати?

How many are there of you/us?
***skeel'**ki vas/nas?* — Скільки вас / нас?

When ...?	***ko**li ...?*	Коли ...?
is our flight	*nash reys*	наш рейс
is the train	***po**yeezd*	поїзд
do we have lunch	*oo nas o**beed***	у нас обід
must I be there	***tre**ba tam **boo**ti*	треба там бути

How is this made?
*yak tse **ro**bit'sya?* — Як це робиться?

Asking Permission

The simplest way of asking permission to do something is to say:

May I?	***mo**zhna?*	Можна?

You can also ask Ви дозволите? *(vi dozvolite?)* which literally means 'Do you permit?' or Ви не заперечуєте? *(vi ne zaperechooyete?)* which means 'You don't object, do you?'.

Responses

Please do.	*tak, **proshoo***	Так, прошу.
Of course.	***zvichayno***	Звичайно.
Unfortunately not.	*na **zhal'**, nee*	На жаль, ні.
I don't want to.	*ya ne **khochoo***	Я не хочу.
I can't.	*ya ne **mozhoo***	Я не можу.
I won't.	*ya ne **boodoo***	Я не буду.

Requests

The following requests are all in the imperative form (command form) of the verb. You should use the polite будь ласка *(bood' laska)* which means 'Please' before the request.

Come in.	***zakhod'te.***	Заходьте.
Give (me) ...	***dayte*** *...*	Дайте …
Pass (me) ...	*pere**dayte** ...*	Передайте …
Show (me) ...	*pokaz**heet'** ...*	Покажіть …
Sit down.	*see**dayte.***	Сідайте.
Take ...	*veez'**meet'** ...*	Візьміть …
Tell (me).	***skazheet'.***	Скажіть.
Translate.	*perekla**deet'**.*	Перекладіть.

SMALL TALK

Getting Around

Public transport in Ukraine is cheap and easy to use, but be prepared for the crowded conditions. Don't be afraid to push – everyone else does! It's a good idea to learn some relevant Cyrillic so you can recognise signs at a glance. Trolleybuses, trams and buses will get you around the cities, and Kyiv and Kharkiv both have metro systems. Taxis are fairly plentiful and cheap by Western standards.

Finding Your Way

Excuse me, where am I?
*vibachte, de ya znak**ho**joosya?* — Вибачте, де я знаходжуся?

What is this place/this street called?
*yak naziv**a**yet'sya tse **mees**tse/tsya **voo**litsya?* — Як називається це місце/ця вулиця?

Where is ...?	*de ...?*	Де ...?
the bus station	*awtovog**zal**/ awto**stan**tseeya*	автовокзал/ автостанція
the train station	*(zaleez**nich**niy) vog**zal***	(залізничний) вокзал
the airport	*aero**port***	аеропорт

the subway station	***stant**seeya metro*	станція метро
the taxi stand	*zoo**pin**ka tak**see***	зупинка таксі
the port	*port*	порт
the ticket office	*(kvit**ko**va) **ka**sa*	(квиткова) каса

Where is Khreshchatyk Street?
*de **voo**litsya Khre**shcha**tik?* Де вулиця Хрещатик?

alley	*pro**voo**lok (prov)*	провулок (пров)
avenue	*pros**pekt** (prosp)*	проспект (просп)
boulevard	*bool'**var** (bool)*	бульвар (бул)
square	***plo**shcha (pl)*	площа (пл)
street	***voo**litsya (vool)*	вулиця (вул)

USEFUL TIP

To ask where something is, say де ...? *(de ...?)* then whatever it is you're looking for.

Refer to page 27

Ukrainian has a number of words for the verb 'to go'. You must be precise about *how* you are going! If you are going on foot the verb is іти *(eeti)*, which you may also see as дійти *(deeyti)*, 'to get to', or прийти *(priyti)*, 'to arrive'. If you are travelling by some means of wheeled transport, the verb is їхати *(yeekhati)*, which may appear in the phrases as доїхати *(doyeekhati)*, 'to get to', or приїхати *(priyeekhati)*, 'to arrive'.

How do I get to ...?	*yak dee**sta**tisya do ...?*	Як дістатися до …?
	yak doyeekhati do ...?	Як доїхати до …?
	*ya**ko**yoo do**ro**hoyoo ...?*	Якою дорогою …?
	*ya **mozhoo** deeyti do ...?*	я можу дійти до …?
the metro	***metro***	метро
the theatre	*te**a**troo*	театру
the museum	*moozeyoo*	музею
the park	***par**koo*	парку

Is it nearby?
*tse **bliz'**ko?* — Це близько?

Is it far?
*tse da**le**ko?* — Це далеко?

How far is it to Desiatynna Street?
*chi daleko **voo**litsya desya**tin**na?* — Чи далеко вулиця Десятинна?

Can I walk there?
*ya **mo**zhoo deey**ti** too**di** **peesh**ki?* — Я можу дійти туди пішки?

Can you show me on the map?
*vi **mo**zhete pokazati (me**nee**) na **kar**tee?* — Ви можете показати (мені) на карті?

How many minutes (walk)?
***skeel'**ki khvi**lin** (ee**ti**)?* — Скільки хвилин (іти)?

What ... is this?	***yaka** tse ...?*	Яка це ...?
street	***voo**litsya*	вулиця
square	***plo**shcha*	площа

The number of the building you are looking for may not always be clearly marked, so make sure you have both building number and flat number. If you are invited to someone's home, you should also ask for the security lock code on the front door of the block:

What is the number of this building?
*yakiy tse **no**mer boo**din**koo?* Який це номер будинку?

What is the code for the security lock?
*ya**kiy** oo vas kod **zam**ka na dver**yakh**?* Який у вас код замка на дверях?

Directions

Go straight ahead.	*eedeet' pryamo*	Ідіть прямо.
Turn left.	*poverneet' leevorooch*	Поверніть ліворуч.
Turn right.	*poverneet' pravorooch*	Поверніть праворуч.
at the corner	*na rozee*	На розі
at the traffic lights	*beelya sveetlofora*	біля світлофора
at the square	*na ploshchee*	на площі
back	*nazad*	назад
up	*whoroo*	вгору
down	*wniz*	вниз
near	*bliz'ko*	близько
far	*daleko*	далеко
under	*peed*	під
over	*nad*	над

Buying Tickets

ДОВІДКОВЕ БЮРО	INFORMATION
КАСА/КАСИ	TICKET OFFICE
КАСИ ПОПЕРЕДНЬОГО ПРОДАЖУ КВИТКІВ	PURCHASE OF TICKETS IN ADVANCE
КВИТКИ	TICKETS
КАМЕРА СХОВУ	LEFT LUGGAGE
ЗАЛ ЧЕКАННЯ	WAITING ROOM

Buy your tickets in advance from kiosks near bus stops. Punch your ticket in the cancelling machine, компостер *(komposter)*, on board the vehicle. If you are going to be in Kyiv for two weeks or more it is probably worthwhile buying a travelcard, проїзний квиток *(proyeezniy kvitok)*. These last for one calendar month, and are valid on all modes of transport in the city.

Excuse me please, where is the ticket office?
*vi**bach**te, bood' **las**ka, de kvit**ko**vee **ka**si?* — Вибачте, будь ласка, де квиткові каси?

Where is the information desk?
*de doveed**ko**ve byoo**ro**?* — Де довідкове бюро?

Where can I buy a bus ticket?
*de **mozh**na koo**pi**ti kvi**tok** na aw**to**boos?* — Де можна купити квиток на автобус?

How much does a ticket cost?
***skeel'**ki **kosh**tooye kvi**tok**?* — Скільки коштує квиток?

Do you have student discounts?
*chi ye **znizh**ka tsee**ni** dlya stoo**den**teew?* — Чи є знижка ціни для студентів?

Please give me (ten) tickets.
day**te, bood' **las**ka, (**de**syat') kvit**keew — Дайте, будь ласка, (десять) квитків.

I'd like ...	*yab kho**teew**/ kho**tee**la ...*	Я б хотів/ хотіла ...
one ticket to ...	***o**din kvi**tok** do ...*	один квиток до ...
two tickets to ...	*dva kvit**ki** do ...*	два квитки до ...
a reservation	*bron'*	бронь
single (ticket)	*kvi**tok** v o**din** beek*	квиток в один бік
return (ticket)	*kvi**tok** too**di** y na**zad**/ zvo**rot**niy kvi**tok***	квиток туди й назад/ зворотний квиток

Can I make a reservation for ... (date)?

***mozh**na zabronyoo**va**ti/ za**mo**viti kvi**tok** na ...?*	Можна забронювати / замовити квиток на ...?

A first-class ticket, please.

*bood' **las**ka, koo**pey**niy (kvi**tok**)*	Будь ласка, купейний (квиток).

A second-class ticket, please.

day**te, bood' **las**ka, plats**kar**tniy kvi**tok	Дайте, будь ласка, плацкартний квиток.

Air

ПРИБУТТЯ	ARRIVALS
ВИДАЧА БАГАЖУ	BAGGAGE CLAIM
ВІДПРАВЛЕННЯ	DEPARTURES
РЕЄСТРАЦІЯ	CHECK-IN
МИТНИЦЯ	CUSTOMS
БЮРО ЗНАХІДОК	LOST PROPERTY
ОБМІН ВАЛЮТИ	MONEY EXCHANGE
ПАСПОРТНИЙ КОНТРОЛЬ	PASSPORT CONTROL

Air travel is well developed throughout Ukraine, although it is often difficult to book seats during peak periods. International flights land at Boryspil International Airport, Бориспіль *(bori**s**peel')*, 40 km south of central Kyiv. Odesa, L'viv and Ivano-Frankivsk airports also handle some international flights.

There are regular bus connections into town. Be wary of accepting a ride in a private car. Zhuliany airport, Жуляни *(zhoolyani)*, is closer to town but is for domestic flights only. Happy landing! – М'якої посадки! ***(myakoyee posadki!)***.

Is there a flight to ...?	
chi ye reys do ...?	Чи є рейс до …?
When is the next flight to ...?	
koli nastoopniy reys do ...?	Коли наступний рейс до…?
What is the flight number?	
yakiy nomer reysoo?	Який номер рейсу?
Where do we check in?	
de reyestratseeya?	Де реєстрація?
When do we have to check in?	
koli pochinayet'sya reyestratseeya na reys?	Коли починається реєстрація на рейс?
One hour/two hours before departure.	
za hodinoo (za dvee hodini) do veedl'otoo	За годину (за дві години) до відльоту.
Where do I check in luggage?	
de mozhna zdati bahazh?	Де можна здати багаж?
Where do I pick up luggage?	
de mozhna oderzhati bahazh?	Де можна одержати багаж?

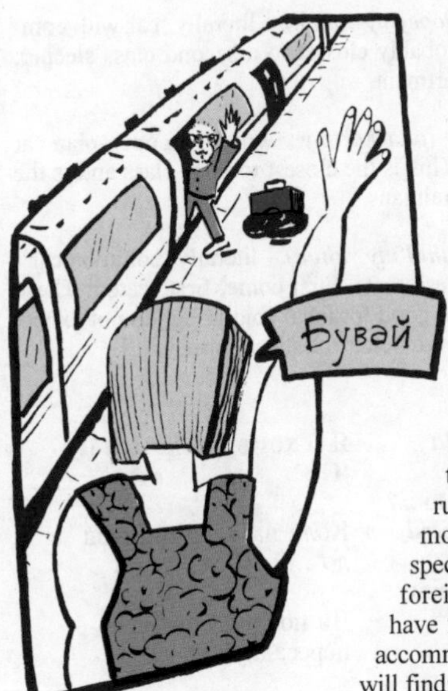

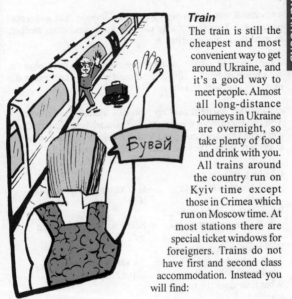

Train

The train is still the cheapest and most convenient way to get around Ukraine, and it's a good way to meet people. Almost all long-distance journeys in Ukraine are overnight, so take plenty of food and drink with you. All trains around the country run on Kyiv time except those in Crimea which run on Moscow time. At most stations there are special ticket windows for foreigners. Trains do not have first and second class accommodation. Instead you will find:

CB *(esve)* – an abbreviation for спальний вагон ***(spal'niy vahon)*** sleeping car. This is the most luxurious and expensive way to travel; two or three berths to a compartment. These carriages may not be available on all long-distance trains.

купейний вагон *(koo**pey**niy va**hon**)* – literally 'car with compartments'. This is probably closest to a second class sleeper; four berths to a compartment.

плацкартний вагон *(plats**kart**niy va**hon**)* – an open-plan car with reserved bunks. This is the closest to third class and is the most popular with Ukrainians.

загальний вагон *(za**hal'**niy va**hon**)* – literally 'common car'. You cannot reserve these seats. First come, first seated! These carriages are cheap and good for local colour, but do not expect to get any sleep. They are better for short journeys.

I'd like a sleeper.	
*yab kho**teew**/kho**tee**la 'esve'*	Я б хотів (m)/хотіла (f) 'СВ'.
When is the next train to ...?	
*ko**li** na**stoop**niy **po**yeezd do ...?*	Коли наступний поїзд до …?
Do I need to change trains?	
*chi po**treeb**no ro**bi**ti pere**sad**koo?*	Чи потрібно робити пересадку?
What time does the train leave?	
*ko**li** veedpraw**lya**yet'sya **po**yeezd?*	Коли відправляється поїзд?
What time does the train arrive?	
*ko**li** **po**yeezd priboo**va**ye?*	Коли поїзд прибуває?

Attention!	*oo**va**ha!*	Увага!
train	***po**yeezd/**po**tyah*	поїзд / потяг

express train	***shvidkiy poyeezd***	швидкий поїзд
stopping train	***pasazhirs'kiy poyeezd***	пасажирський поїзд
local train	***(primees'kiy) elektropoyeezd/ elektrichka***	(приміський) електропоїзд / електричка
car/carriage	***vahon***	вагон
kiosk	***keeosk***	кіоск
railway station	***zaleeznichna stantseeya/vogzal***	залізнична станція / вокзал
timetable	***rozklad (rookhoo poyeezdeew)***	розклад (руху поїздів)
platform	***platforma***	платформа

Bus, Tram & Trolleybus

Due to frequent fuel shortages, buses can be unreliable. Trams and trolleybuses offer a better service as they run on electricity but they can become extremely crowded.

A	Bus Stop	Tp	Trolleybus Stop
T	Tram Stop	M	Metro

bus	***awtoboos***	автобус
tram (trolley)	***tramvay***	трамвай
trolleybus	***troleyboos***	тролейбус

Where is the nearest bus stop?
*de nay**blizh**cha awto**boos**na zoo**pin**ka?* — Де найближча автобусна зупинка?

Which bus goes to ...?
*ya**kiy** awto**boos** ee**de** do ...?* — Який автобус іде до …?

Can you tell me when we get to ...?
*vi **mo**zhete me**nee** ska**za**ti, de vi**kho**diti?* — Ви можете мені сказати, де виходити?

Can you tell me where we are?
*ska**zheet'**, bood' **las**ka, de mi **za**raz?* — Скажіть, будь ласка, де ми зараз?

What stop is this?
*ya**ka** tse zoo**pin**ka?* — Яка це зупинка?

If you find yourself on a crowded vehicle, the following phrases will be useful:

Excuse me, I'd like to get off!
*doz**vol'**te (proy**ti**)* — Дозвольте (пройти)
(lit: allow me to pass)
*vi **za**raz vi**kho**dite?* — Ви зараз виходите?
(lit: are you getting off now?)
*vi vi**kho**dite na nas**toop**neey (zoo**pin**tsee)?* — Ви виходите на наступній (зупинці)?
(lit: are you getting off at the next stop?)

Please pass this ticket to be punched.
*pere**day**te na kom**pos**ter* — Передайте на компостер.

Please tell the driver to stop.
*popro**seet'** vo**dee**ya zoopi**ni**tisya* — Попросіть водія зупинитися.

USEFUL TIP

To attract someone's attention when you want to ask a question, say Можна? *(mozhna?)* which means 'May I?'. It's also the simplest way of asking permission.

Refer to page 31

Metro

Kyiv and Kharkiv both have metro systems. A flat fare system operates; simply buy your token, жетон *(zheton),* at the booth in the station and insert it into the slot on the entrance gate.

Where is the nearest metro station?
*de nay**blizh**cha **stan**tseeya met**ro**?* — Де найближча станція метро?

Where do I purchase tokens for the metro?
*de **mozh**na koo**pi**ti zhe**to**ni na met**ro**?* — Де можна купити жетони на метро?

How much does a token cost?
skeel'ki koshtooye zheton? — Скільки коштує жетон?

Does this train go to ...?
tsey poyeezd eede do ...? — Цей поїзд іде до ...?

Which station is this?
yaka tse stantseeya? — Яка це станція?

What metro line is this?
yaka tse leeneeya metro? — Яка це лінія метро?

Taxi

Taxi ranks are clearly marked. Taxis are metered, but in these days of galloping inflation they do not offer much indication as to what you will have to pay. Sometimes there is a handwritten notice next to the meter inviting you to multiply the amount shown by 13,000 or even more. A pocket calculator is useful.

A word of warning: many drivers of private cars supplement their income by cruising the streets in search of people wanting to get somewhere in a hurry. It is always best to use official taxis only. If you do use a private car, think twice about getting in if there is anyone else in the car beside the driver.

taxi	*taksee*	таксі

I want to go to ...
*menee **treba yeekhati** do ...* — Мені треба їхати до …
How much is it to ...?
***skeel'ki** do ...?* — Скільки до …?
How much do I owe you?
***skeel'ki** (z **mene**)?* — Скільки (з мене)?

Take me ...	*peedvezeet' mene ...*	Підвезіть мене …
to the airport	*v aero**port***	в аеропорт
to the port	*oo **port***	у порт
to the station	*na **stan**tseeyoo*	на станцію
to a cheap hotel	*oo de**she**viy **hotel'***	у дешевий готель

Instructions

Slow down!
*prihal'**mooy**te!* — Пригальмуйте!

A little further. *__tro__khi __da__lee*	Трохи далі.
Turn left. *pover__neet’__ lee__vo__rooch*	Поверніть ліворуч.
Turn right. *pover__neet’__ pra__vo__rooch*	Поверніть праворуч.
Into this street. *oo tsyoo __voo__litsyoo*	У цю вулицю.
Round the corner. *za povo__ro__tom*	За поворотом.
Just by the trolleybus stop. *bee__lya__ tro__ley__boosnoyee zoo__pin__ki*	Біля тролейбусної зупинки.
Please stop here. *(zoopi__neet’__sya) toot, bood’ __las__ka*	(Зупиніться) тут, будь ласка.
Please wait for a minute. *zache__kay__te, bood’ __las__ka, khvi__lin__koo*	Зачекайте, будь ласка, хвилинку.

Boat

When is the next boat to (Odesa)? *__ko__li na__stoop__niy paro__plaw__ do (o__de__si)?*	Коли наступний пароплав до (Одеси)?
How many hours is it to (Zaporizhzhya)? *__skeel’__ki ho__din__ do (zapo__reezh__zhya)?*	Скільки годин до (Запоріжжя)?

Does the boat stop at (Kaniv)?
*chi paro**plaw ro**bit' zoo**pin**koo w (**ka**nevee)?* Чи пароплав робить зупинку в (Каневі)?

What time does the boat depart/arrive?
*o kot**reey** hodi**nee** paro**plaw** veedpli**va**ye/pripli**va**ye?* О котрій годині пароплав відпливає/припливає?

Where does the boat depart from?
***zveed**ki paro**plaw** veedpli**va**ye?* Звідки пароплав відпливає?

Car

You can hire just about any make of car in Ukraine, with or without a driver, especially in Kyiv. It is, however, not cheap, and long-distance driving is only for the very adventurous, especially in winter. Taking your own car can be fun, that is if you are willing to run the risk of a long wait at the border, you have a large jerry can (or preferably several) that you can keep full of petrol and you are confident about your skills with engines in case you have a breakdown. Outside the towns, petrol stations are few and far between.

СТОЯНКА ЗАБОРОНЕНА	NO PARKING

car	*ma**shi**na/ awtomo**beel'***	машина/ автомобіль

Where can I hire a car?
*de **mozh**na nay**nya**ti ma**shi**noo/awtomo**beel'**?* Де можна найняти машину/автомобіль?

How much does it cost per day?
*skeel'ki **kosh**tooye prokat oo den'?* — Скільки коштує прокат у день?

How much does it cost per week?
***skeel'**ki platiti w **tizh**den'?* — Скільки платити в тиждень?

Is insurance included?
*chi tse wklyoo**cha**ye stra**khow**koo?* — Чи це включає страховку?

Give me ... litres of petrol/ gasoline.
***day**te, bood' **las**ka, ... **leet**reew (**leet**ri) ben**zi**noo* — Дайте, будь ласка, ... літрів (літри) бензину.

Fill it up.
*zapow**neet'**/za**liy**te* — Заповніть/залийте.

Can you tell me the way to ...?
*peedka**zheet'** do**ro**hoo do .../ vi ne **ska**zhete, yak do**yee**khati do ...?* — Підкажіть дорогу до .../ Ви не скажете, як доїхати до ...?

Are we on the right road to ...?
*mi **pra**vil'no **yee**demo do .../chi tse **pra**vil'na do**ro**ha do ...?* — Ми правильно їдемо до .../Чи це правильна дорога до ...?

How far is it to ...?
*chi da**le**ko do ...?* — Чи далеко до ...?

Is it OK to park here?
*toot **mozh**na posta**vi**ti ma**shi**noo?* — Тут можна поставити машину?

Car Problems

Can you help me?
*dopomo**zheet'**, bood' **las**ka*
Допоможіть, будь ласка.

How far is the next service station?
*chi daleko (zveedsi) awtoser**vees**?*
Чи далеко (звідси) автосервіс?

Where is the nearest petrol/gas station?
*de nay**blizh**cha za**praw**ka?*
Де найближча заправка?

My car has broken down. *oo **me**ne polama**la**sya ma**shi**na*	У мене поламалася машина.
I need to change a wheel. *me**nee** **tre**ba pomee**nya**ti ko**le**so*	Мені треба поміняти колесо.

Paperwork

Name	*ee**mya***	Ім'я
Surname	***pree**zvishche*	Прізвище
Patronymic	*po-**bat'**kovee*	По-батькові
Address	*a**dre**sa*	Адреса
work	*sloozh**bo**va*	службова
home	*do**mash**nya*	домашня
telephone	*tele**fon***	Телефон
Date of birth	***da**ta naro**jen**nya*	Дата народження
Place of birth	***mees**tse naro**jen**nya*	Місце народження
Age	*veek*	Вік
Sex	*stat'*	Стать
Profession	*pro**fe**seeya*	Професія
Place of employment	***mees**tse ro**bo**ti*	Місце роботи
Position held	*po**sa**da*	Посада
Passport number	***no**mer **pas**porta*	Номер паспорта
Birth certificate	*svee**dots**tvo pro naro**jen**nya*	Свідоцтво про народження
Driver's licence	*pra**va** vo**dee**ya*	Права водія
Car registration certificate	*tekh**neech**niy **pas**port*	Технічний паспорт
Car registration number	*reyestra**tsee**yniy **no**mer ma**shi**ni*	Реєстраційний номер машини

Accommodation

Ukraine is only now discovering its potential as a tourist destination. The iron grip of the erstwhile Soviet foreign tourist organisation, Intourist, is no longer as firm as it was, but there has been little investment since independence in the development of cheap hotels with high standards. When the Soviet Union existed, tourists could obtain a visa only on the basis of pre-booked accommodation. The rules are now much less stringent.

Wherever you stay it is highly likely that you will be charged more than a citizen of Ukraine. If you're planning to stay in one place for a long period, particularly in Kyiv, it might be worth considering renting a flat or a room in a private home. There are agencies that can make these arrangements for you.

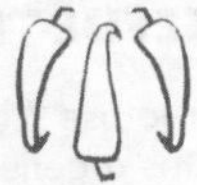

Can you tell me where there is ...?	*ska**zheet'**, bood' **las**ka, de ...?*	Скажіть, будь ласка, де …?
a good hotel	***har**niy ho**tel'***	гарний готель
a cheap hotel	*de**she**viy ho**tel'***	дешевий готель
a youth hostel	*molo**deezh**niy hoor**to**zhitok*	молодіжний гуртожиток
a tourist office	*tooris**tich**ne byoo**ro***	туристичне бюро
a camp site	***kem**peenh*	кемпінг

Renting

I am looking for accommodation in the centre.
*ya shoo**ka**yoo zhit**lo** w **tsen**tree* — Я шукаю житло в центрі.

I want to rent a flat.
*ya **kho**choo nay**nya**ti kvar**ti**roo* — Я хочу найняти квартиру.

I need a (one-roomed/two-roomed) flat with telephone.
*me**nee** po**treeb**na (odnokeem**nat**na/ dvokeem**nat**na) kvar**ti**ra z tele**fo**nom* — Мені потрібна (однокімнатна / двокімнатна) квартира з телефоном.

USEFUL TIP

Remember to use Добридень (*dobriden'*) as a general 'Hello'.

Refer to page 29

At the Hotel

When you check in you are likely to be asked for your passport. This is a police requirement for registration purposes. It should be returned to you within 24 hours. If it is not, ask for it. You will also have to fill out an information form. (See Paperwork, page 72.)

Checking In

Do you have any free rooms?
*oo vas ye **veel'**nee no**me**ri?* — У вас є вільні номери?

I need a room.
menee potreebniy nomer — Мені потрібний номер.

I want to book a room.
ya khochoo zabronyoovati nomer — Я хочу забронювати номер.

A room has been reserved for me.
dlya mene zamowleno nomer — Для мене замовлено номер.

You should have a reservation in the name of ... .
oo vas maye booti zamowlennya na preezvishche ... — У вас має бути замовлення на прізвище …

I'd like a ...	*yab khoteew/ khoteela ...*	Я б хотів (m)/ хотіла (f) ...
single room	*nomer na odnoho*	номер на одного
double room	*nomer na dvokh*	номер на двох
shared room	*meestse*	місце

I'd like a room ...	*yab khoteew/ khoteela nomer ...*	Я б хотів (m)/ хотіла номер (f)...
with shower and toilet	*z dooshem ee tooaletom*	з душем і туалетом
with a telephone	*z telefonom*	з телефоном
with a refrigerator	*z kholodil'nikom*	з олодильником
with a television	*z televeezorom*	з телевізором
with a balcony	*z balkonom*	з балконом

How much is the room ...?	***skeel'ki kosh**tooye **no**mer ...?*	Скільки коштує номер …?
per night	*za neech*	за ніч
for ... nights	*za ... **no**chee/ no**chey***	за … ночі / ночей
per week	*oo **tizh**den'*	у тиждень

Can I see the room?
***mozh**na podi**vi**tisya **no**mer?* — Можна подивитися номер?

Is breakfast included?
*chi tse wklyoo**cha**ye **var**teest' snee**dan**koo?* — Чи це включає вартість сніданку?

What time do I have to check out?
***ko**li ya po**vi**nen/po**vin**na zveel'**ni**ti **no**mer?* — Коли я повинен / повинна звільнити номер?

What is the room number?
*ya**kiy** tse **no**mer?* — Який це номер?

What floor is that?
*ya**kiy** tse **po**verkh?* — Який це поверх?

I'll take it. (this room)
*ya be**roo** (tsey **no**mer)* — Я беру. (цей номер)

Complaints

Do you have another room?
*oo vas ye **een**shiy **no**mer?* — У вас є інший номер?

The shower/tap doesn't work.
*doosh/kran ne **pra**tsyooye* — Душ / кран не працює.

The tap drips.
*kran protee**ka**ye* — Кран протікає.

There is no hot water.
*ne**ma**ye ha**rya**choyee vodi* — Немає гарячої води.

I've got a broken ... in my room.	*oo **no**meree polamane ...*	У номері поламане …
bed	***leezh**ko*	ліжко
radio	***ra**deeo*	радіо
light switch	*vimi**kach***	вимикач
television	*televeezorom*	телевізором

There's no light bulb in my room.
*oo **me**ne ne**ma**ye **lam**pochki* — У мене немає лампочки.

There's no toilet paper in my room.
*oo **me**ne ne**ma**ye tooa**let**noho pa**pe**roo* — У мене немає туалетного паперу.

I can't open/close the window.
*vee**kno** ne veedchi**nya**yet'sya/zachi**nya**yet'sya* — Вікно не відчиняється / зачиняється.

It's too cold.
*toot **doo**zhe **kho**lodno* — Тут дуже холодно.

It's too hot.
*toot **doo**zhe **zhar**ko* — Тут дуже жарко.

It's very noisy.
*toot **doo**zhe **shoom**no* — Тут дуже шумно.

The room is dirty.
*oo **no**meree **brood**no* — У номері брудно.

There are bugs in the bed.
*oo **leezh**koo blo**shchi**tsee* — У ліжку блощиці.

Requests

Can I leave my valuables here?
chi ya ***mozh****oo zali****shi****ti svo****yee*** *kosh****tow****nee* ***re****chee toot?*
Чи я можу залишити свої коштовні речі тут?

I'd like to make a phone call.
*yab kho****teew****/kho****tee****la podzvo****ni****ti*
Я б хотів (m)/хотіла (f) подзвонити.

I'd like to book an international telephone call.
*yab kho****teew****/kho****tee****la za****mo****viti meezhna****rod****noo roz****mo****voo*
Я б хотів (m)/ хотіла (f) замовити міжнародну розмову.

Can I have ...? *mozhna wzyati/ dayte bood' laska ...* Можна взяти/ Дайте будь ласка ...

- my key — *meey klyooch* — мій ключ
- my luggage — *meey bahazh* — мій багаж
- the account — *rakhoonok* — рахунок

Could you call me a taxi?
vi mozhete viklikati dlya mene taksee? Ви можете викликати для мене таксі?

USEFUL TIP

Remember to use Можна? (*mozhna?*) before any request you make.

Refer to page 50

Checking Out

We're checking out ... *mi viyeezhjayemo/ mi vipisooyemosya...* Ми виїжджаємо/ Ми виписуємося ...

- today — *s'ohodnee* — сьогодні
- tonight — *s'ohodnee oovecheree* — сьогодні увечері
- tomorrow — *zawtra* — завтра

Can I leave my luggage here?
ya mozhoo zalishiti toot sveey bahazh? Я можу залишити тут свій багаж?

Laundry

There are no self-service laundries but some hotels may be able to offer a laundry service. Finding a drycleaner is much easier.

Can I get things laundered?
*chi **mozh**na zdavati **re**chee oo pran**nya**?* — Чи можна здавати речі у прання?

Is there a washing machine I can use?
*chi toot ye **pral'na** ma**shi**na, ya**ko**yoo **mozh**na koristoo**va**tisya?* — Чи тут є пральна машина, якою можна користуватися?

Do you have washing powder?
*oo vas ye **pral'**niy poro**shok**?* — У вас є пральний порошок?

How do I switch it on?
*yak yee**yee** ooveem**knoo**ti?* — Як її увімкнути?

The washing machine doesn't work.
***pral'**na ma**shi**na ne prats**yoo**ye* — Пральна машина не працює.

Where is there a laundry/ drycleaners?
*de zna**kho**dit'sya **pral'**nya/ kheem**chist**ka?* — Де знаходиться пральня/ хімчистка?

It's urgent.
*tse termi**no**vo* — Це терміново.

When can I get it/them back?
*ko**li** **mozh**na za**bra**ti/ o**der**zhati?* — Коли можна забрати/ одержати?

Some Useful Phrases

Where can I do some ironing?
*a de **mozh**na prasoo**va**ti?* А де можна прасувати?

When is the restaurant open?
*ko**li** pratsyoo**ye** resto**ran**?* Коли працює ресторан?

When is the bedlinen changed?
*ko**li** mee**nya**yoot' beeliz**noo**?* Коли міняють білизну?

At what time is the room cleaned?
*o ko**triy** hodi**nee** pribi**ran**nya?* О котрій годині прибирання?

Can I have my passport please?
*chi ya **mo**zhoo wzya**ti** sveey **pa**sport?* Чи я можу взяти свій паспорт?

Where can I find the duty manager?
*de **mozh**na znay**ti** admeeneest**ra**tora?* Де можна знайти адміністратора?

Where's your phone?
*de oo vas tele**fon**?* Де у вас телефон?

Where's the lift?
de toot lift? Де тут ліфт?

Some Useful Words

adaptor	*perekheed**nik***	перехідник
alarm clock	*boo**dil'**nik*	будильник
bed	***leezh**ko*	ліжко
bedlinen	*po**steel**'na beeliz**na***	постільна білизна
blanket	***kow**dra*	ковдра
chair	*stee**lets'***	стілець

clean	***chis**tiy*	чистий
dirty	***brood**niy*	брудний
door	*dve**ree***	двері (pl)
door handle	***rooch**ka*	ручка
electrical socket	*elek**trich**na rozetka*	едектрична розетка
fan	*venti**lya**tor*	вентилятор
heating	*o**pa**lennya*	опалення
iron	***pras**ka*	праска
light	***svee**tlo*	світло
lightswitch	*vimi**kach***	вимикач
lock	*za**mok***	замок
mirror	***dzer**kalo*	дзеркало
pillow	*po**doosh**ka*	подушка
pillowcase	***na**volochka*	наволочка
sleeping bag	***spal'**niy mee**shok***	спальний мішок
suitcase	*va**lee**za*	валіза
table	*steel*	стіл
shelf	*po**li**tsya*	полиця
sheets	*prosti**rad**la*	простирадла
soap	***mi**lo*	мило
tap/faucet	*kran*	кран
toilet	*tooa**let***	туалет
toilet paper	*tooa**let**niy pa**peer***	туалетний папір
towel	*roosh**nik***	рушник
washbasin	*oomi**val'**nik*	умивальник
window	*veek**no***	вікно
wet	***mok**riy*	мокрий

Around Town

At the Bank

The Ukrainian unit of currency is the *karbovanets*, карбованець *(kar**bo**vanets')*, also referred to as a coupon, купон *(koo**pon**)*. There are plans to introduce a completely new currency unit called the *hryvna*, гривна *(**hri**wna)*, when the economic climate permits. It is now against the law to use currencies other than Ukrainian karbovantsy to pay for goods and services, except in clearly marked establishments.

You will have no difficulties changing US dollars or deutschmark, provided you have small denominations and clean notes. Banknotes with writing on them are almost always rejected in Ukraine. Don't be tempted by exchange offers from individuals in the street. You run the risk of being ripped off – it's not difficult to cut pieces of paper to size and insert them between real banknotes!

Personal cheques are generally not accepted and as yet there are no magic holes in walls from which money can be obtained. The majority of hotels and restaurants and quite a few shops will accept major credit cards.

БАНК	BANK
ОБМІН ВАЛЮТИ	CURRENCY EXCHANGE
ПУНКТ ОБМІНУ ВАЛЮТИ	CURRENCY EXCHANGE POINT
КАСИР	CASHIER
КЕРІВНИК/МЕНЕДЖЕР	MANAGER

Do you change travellers' cheques?	*vi mee**nya**yete do**rozh**nee **che**ki?*	Ви міняєте дорожні чеки?
What is the exchange rate?	*ya**kiy** koors (**ob**meenoo val**yoo**ti)?*	Який курс (обміну валюти)?
I'd like to change ...	*ya b kho**teew**/kho**tee**la obmee**nya**ti ...*	Я б хотів (m)/хотіла (f) обміняти ...
a travellers' cheque	*do**rozh**niy chek*	дорожній чек
this money into karbovantsy	*tsee **hro**shee na kar**bo**vantsee*	ці гроші на карбованці
100 dollars/pounds/deutschmarks	*sto **do**lareew/**foon**teew/**ma**rok*	сто доларів/фунтів/марок

How many ... will that be?
__skeel'__ki ... tse __boo__de? — Скільки … це буде?

Could you write that down?
vi __mo__zhete tse zapi__sa__ti/ napi__sheet'__ tse, bood' __las__ka? — Ви можете це записати/ Напишіть це, будь ласка?

Can I have some money transferred to here?
chi __mozh__na pereves__ti__ mo__yee__ __hro__shee syoo__di__? — Чи можна перевести мої гроші сюди?
chi __mozh__na zro__bi__ti hrosho__viy__ pe__re__kaz? — Чи можна зробити грошовий переказ?

How long will it take?
__skeel'__ki __cha__soo tse zay__me__? — Скільки часу це займе?

Have you received my money order yet?
chi vi o__der__zhali meey hrosho__viy__ pe__re__kaz? — Чи ви одержали мій грошовий переказ?

Could I speak to the manager?
chi __mozh__na pohovo__ri__ti z kereewni__kom__? — Чи можна поговорити з керівником?

USEFUL TIP

If you're having trouble making yourself understood, turn to page 47.

deutschmark	*nee__mets'__kee __mar__ki*	німецькі марки
yen	*ya__pons__'kee ee__ye__ni*	японські ієни
UK pounds	*an__hleeys__'kee __foon__ti __ster__leenheew*	англійські фунти стерлінгів

AROUND TOWN

US dollars	*amerikans'kee dolari*	американські долари
banknote	*banknota/koopyoora*	банкнота / купюра
signature	*peedpis*	підпис
sum	*sooma*	сума
in figures	*tsiframi*	цифрами
in words	*propisom*	прописом
personal cheques	*osobistee cheki*	особисті чеки
travellers' cheques	*dorozhnee cheki*	дорожні чеки

At the Post Office

ПОШТА	POST OFFICE
ПОШТОВЕ ВІДДІЛЕННЯ	POSTAL SERVICES
ЦЕНТРАЛЬНИЙ ПОШТАМТ	CENTRAL POST OFFICE
ГОЛОВПОШТАМТ	MAIN POST OFFICE
ПОШТА	POST
ТЕЛЕФОН	TELEPHONE
ТЕЛЕГРАФ	TELEGRAPH
ЕКСПРЕС-ПОШТА	EXPRESS MAIL
ЛИСТИ НА ЗАМОВЛЕННЯ	REGISTERED MAIL
ПОСИЛКИ	PARCELS
ГРОШОВІ ПЕРЕКАЗИ	MONEY ORDERS
ВІДПРАВЛЕННЯ ФАКСОВИХ ПОВ-ІДОМЛЕНЬ	FAX SERVICE
МІСЦЕВА КОРЕСПОНДЕНЦІЯ	LOCAL MAIL
ОДЕРЖАННЯ КОРЕСПОНДЕНЦІЇ	POSTE RESTANTE

Where is the post office?	
*de **posh**ta?*	Де пошта?
What time does the post office open?	
*koli pra**tsyoo**ye **posh**ta?*	Коли працює пошта?
Where is the nearest letterbox?	
*de nay**blizh**cha posh**to**va **skrin'**ka?*	Де найближча поштова скринька?
I'd like to send this letter to (Australia).	
*me**nee** po**treeb**no nadee**sla**ti **lis**ta do (aw**stra**leeyee).*	Мені потрібно надіслати листа до (Австралії).
How much is a stamp (within Kyiv/within Ukraine)?	
***skeel'**ki **kosh**tooye **mar**ka (w **me**zhakh **ki**yeva/w **me**zhakh ookra**yee**ni)?*	Скільки коштує марка (в межах Києва/в межах України)?

I want to send a letter ...	*ya **kho**choo nadee**sla**ti **lis**ta ...*	Я хочу надіслати листа…
by airmail	*aveea**posh**toyoo*	авіапоштою
by regular mail	*zvi**chay**noyoo **posh**toyoo*	звичайною поштою
registered	*na za**mow**lennya*	на замовлення
by express mail	*eks**pres-posh**toyoo*	експрес-поштою

I want to send a fax.	
*ya **kho**choo veed**pra**viti faks*	Я хочу відправити факс.
How much does it cost per minute?	
***skeel'**ki **kosh**tooye khvi**li**na?*	Скільки коштує хвилина?

AROUND TOWN

Do I have any mail?
*dlya **me**ne ye **posh**ta?* Для мене є пошта?

address	*a**dre**sa*	адреса
aerogramme	*aero**hra**ma*	аерограма
envelope	*kon**vert***	конверт
letter	*list*	лист
padded bag	***pa**ket eez pro**klad**koyoo*	пакет із прокладкою
pen	***rooch**ka*	ручка
pencil	*olee**vets'***	олівець
post code	*(**posh**to**viy) **een**deks*	(поштовий) індекс
postal order	***posh**to**ve** za**mow**lennya*	поштове замовлення
postcard	*lis**teew**ka*	листівка
receipt	*chek/kvi**tan**tseeya/ roz**pis**ka pro oder**zhannya*	чек / квитанція / розписка про одержання
stamp (postage)	***mar**ka*	марка
stamp (rubber)	*shtamp/pe**chat**ka*	штамп / печатка
telegram	*tele**hra**ma*	телеграма
telegram form	*blank (tele**hra**mi)*	бланк (телеграми)

Telephone

The telephone service in Ukraine is improving rapidly. However you may find that you still have to book long-distance and international calls through the operator. Public phones (if they are working) can be used for free local calls only – perhaps the only benefit of a rate of inflation that has led to the complete absence of coins in circulation. Telephones that accept phonecards are being introduced. Long-distance and international calls can be made from main post offices and railway stations.

You may see the mysterious word ТАКСОФОН on some public phones. In the old days, when you needed a coin to make a phone call, these phones would cut you off when a certain amount of time had passed.

ТЕЛЕФОН	TELEPHONE
ТЕЛЕФОНИ-АВТОМАТИ	PUBLIC TELEPHONES
МІЖМІСЬКИЙ ТЕЛЕФОН	LONG-DISTANCE TELEPHONE
МІЖМІСЬКИЙ ПЕРЕГОВОРНИЙ ПУНКТ	LONG-DISTANCE CALLS CAN BE MADE HERE
ТЕЛЕФОННА КАРТКА	PHONECARD

How much does it cost per minute?
*skeel'ki **kosh**tooye khvilina?* Скільки коштує хвилина?

I'd like to make a call to (Ireland).
*menee po**treeb**no podzvo**ni**ti do (eer**lan**deeyee)* Мені потрібно подзвонити до (Ірландії).

I'd like to book a call to (Canada).
*ya **kho**choo za**mo**viti roz**mo**voo z (ka**na**doyoo)* Я хочу замовити розмову з (Канадою).

What is the country code for (Singapore)?
*ya**kiy** kod (sinha**poo**roo)?* Який код (Сингапуру)?

What is the overseas access code?
*shcho **tre**ba na**bra**ti **pe**red **no**merom dlya meezhna**rod**-noho dzveen**ka**?* Що треба набрати перед номером для міжнарод-ного дзвінка?

Do you have a telephone directory?
*oo vas ye tele**fon**niy dovee**dnik**/tele**fon**na **kni**ha?* У вас є телефонний довідник / телефонна книга?

I got the wrong number.
*ya pomi**li**wsya/pomi**li**lasya **no**merom* Я помилився / помилилася номером.

We were cut off.
*nas rozyed**na**li* Нас роз'єднали.

You Might Hear

The number is engaged.
zaynyato — Зайнято.

Will you wait?
boodete chekati? — Будете чекати?

Do you want me to try again?
powtoriti zamowlennya? — Повторити замовлення?

There's no reply.
nomer ne veedpoveedaye — Номер не відповідає.

There's no dial tone.
nemaye hoodkeew — Немає гудків.

Telephone Talk

Hello!
dobriden' — Добридень!

I'd like to speak to ... .
poproseet', bood' laska, do telefonoo ... — Попросіть, будь ласка, до телефону …
(lit: please ask ... to the phone.)

mozhna poprositi do telefonoo ... ? — Можна попросити до телефону …?
(lit: may I ask ... to the phone?)

skazheet', bood' laska, ye ...? — Скажіть, будь ласка, є …?
(lit: tell me, please, is ... there?)

chi ya mozhoo hovoriti z ...? — Чи я можу говорити з …?
(lit: may I speak with ...?)

This is ... speaking.
tse hovorit'/dzvonit' ... — Це говорить/дзвонить ...

This is ... troubling you.
vas toorbooye ... . — Вас турбує ...

Does someone there speak English?
chi khtos' hovorit' anhliys'koyoo movoyoo? — Чи хтось говорить англійською мовою?

Could I have extension number ...?
mozhna dodatkoviy (nomer) ... ? — Можна додатковий (номер) ...?
bood' laska, vnootreeshneey (nomer) ... . — Будь ласка, внутрішній (номер) ... .

Could you speak more loudly?
vi mozhete hovoriti holosneeshe? — Ви можете говорити голосніше?

I'm sorry, I can't hear you.
pereproshooyoo, vas ne chooti. — Перепрошую, вас не чути.

I'll call again.
ya (vam) peredzvonyoo. — Я (вам) передзвоню.

Some Useful Words

code	*kod*	код
number	*nomer*	номер
phone box	*telefon-awtomat*	телефон-автомат
receiver	*troobka*	трубка
ringing tone	*hoodok*	гудок
subscriber	*abonent*	абонент
token	*zheton*	жетон

Sightseeing

Ukrainian cities are rich with museums. In Kyiv most museums have English-speaking guides. Kyiv is well-known for its historical sites, but L'viv, with its baroque churches, is also waiting for you. The world has yet to discover the Carpathian mountains, Карпати *(karpaty)*, in the west and the marshlands of Polisse, Полісся *(poleessya)*, in the north-west. Visit places with evocative names like Kamianets'-Podil'skiy, Камянець-Подільський ***(kamyanets'-podeel'skiy)***, and the Crimean Tatar town of Bakhchisaray, Бахчисарай *(bakhchisaray)*, and its fountain of love. The ancient Greek city of Khersones, Херсонес *(khersones)*, is unfortunately within the boundaries of the modern(ish) port of Sevastopol, a place where even citizens of Ukraine require a special pass to go to – presumably so that profane eyes may not gaze upon the rusting hulks of the former Soviet Black Sea fleet, but that is another story.

I want to go on an excursion.

*ya **kho**choo peeti/ poyeekhati na ekskoorseeyoo*	Я хочу піти / поїхати на екскурсію.

How much is the entry fee?

***ya**ka **pla**ta za wkheed?*	Яка плата за вхід?

Is there a student discount?

*chi ye **znizh**ki/**peel'**hi dlya stoo**den**teew?*	Чи є знижки / пільги для студентів?

Is there an English-speaking guide?

*oo vas ye **anhlo**mowniy ekskoorso**vod**?*	У вас є англомовний екскурсовод?

May I take photographs?

*toot **mozh**na fotohrafoovati?*	Тут можна фтографувати?

What are the opening hours?

***ko**li toot veed**chi**neno?*	Коли тут відчинено?

What time does it close?

***ko**li oo vas zachi**nya**yoot'?*	Коли у вас зачиняють?

It's ...	*tse ...*	Це ...
beautiful	***har**no*	гарно
impressive	*wra**zha**ye*	вражає
interesting	*tsee**ka**vo*	цікаво
magnificent	*choo**do**vo*	чудово
strange	***diw**no*	дивно

AROUND TOWN

antiquity	***pa**myatka*	пам'ятка
	*starovi**ni***	старовини
art gallery	*kar**tin**na hale**re**ya*	картинна галерея
cathedral	*so**bor***	собор
church	***tserk**va*	церква
monastery	*monas**tir***	монастир
monument	***pa**myatnik*	пам'ятник
museum	*moo**zey***	музей
tourist office	*ekskoor**seey**ne byoo**ro**/toorbyoo**ro** (tooris**tich**ne byoo**ro**)*	екскурсійне бюро / турбюро (туристичне бюро)

Entertainment

Nightclubs with an international appeal are only just beginning to develop. Going dancing in a restaurant is a much more popular pastime than in the West. Larger cities have many theatre performances at low prices.

I'd like to go ...	*ya **khochoo peeti** ...*	Я хочу піти …
to a movie	*do/w kee**no***	до / в кіно
to the theatre	*do te**a**troo*	до театру
to the circus	*do **tsir**koo*	до цирку
to a football match	*na foot**bol'**niy match*	на футбольний матч
to a nightclub	*oo neech**niy** kloob*	у нічний клуб
to a concert	*na kon**tsert***	на концерт

Do you have a table free?
*oo vas ye **veel'**niy **sto**lik?* У вас є вільний столик?
Is there live music?
*toot **hra**ye (zhi**va**) **moo**zika?* Тут грає (жива) музика?
Is the movie in English?
*tsey feel'm an**hleeys**'koyoo **mo**voyoo?* Цей фільм англійською мовою?
Could I have two tickets?
mozh**na dva kvit**ki Можна два квитки.
***day**te dva kvit**ki**.* Дайте два квитки.

USEFUL TIP

It's best to always address people you have just met with the more polite form of 'you' - ви *(vi)*. Use the more familiar 'you' - ти *(ti)* - if you are invited to do so.

Refer to page 17

Signs

ДОВІДКА (ДОВІДКОВЕ БЮРО)	INFORMATION
ЗАЧИНЕНО	CLOSED
ВІДЧИНЕНО	OPEN
ВХІД	ENTRY
ВИХІД	EXIT
НЕМАЄ ВХОДУ	NO ENTRY
НЕМАЄ ВИХОДУ	NO EXIT
ДО СЕБЕ	PULL
ВІД СЕБЕ	PUSH
ДО ...	TO ...
ПЕРЕХІД	PEDESTRIAN CROSSING
МІЛІЦІЯ	POLICE
ЗАБОРОНЕНО	PROHIBITED
ТУАЛЕТ	TOILET
НЕ ПАЛИТИ	NO SMOKING
ОБЕРЕЖНО	BE CAREFUL!
НЕ ДОТОРКАТИСЯ!	DON'T TOUCH!

In the Country

Weather

In summer the temperature can climb to 35° C. If you prefer the cold, go in winter when the temperature can range from -2° right down to -30°. The thermometer manages to climb to just above zero in March and November – bring an umbrella. Spring is in the air in April but there can be sharp changes in temperature. The best months for a visit are undoubtedly May and September. It's warm, but not too hot, and it doesn't rain very often. Moreover the lilac and the chestnut trees for which Kyiv is famous are in bloom. 'Come to Kyiv in May.' – Приїжджайте до Києва в травні. *(priyeezh**jay**te do **ki**yeva w **traw**nee)*

It's hot.	***zhar**ko*	Жарко.
It's humid.	***si**ro*	Сиро.
It's damp.	*vo**lo**ho*	Волого.
It's cold.	***kho**lodno*	Холодно.
It's chilly.	*prokho**lo**dno*	Прохолодно.
It's windy (outside).	*na **voo**litsee **vee**ter*	На вулиці вітер.
It's snowing.	*ee**de** sneeh*	Іде сніг.
It's raining.	*ee**de** doshch*	Іде дощ.
It's sunny.	*s'**o**hodnee **so**nyachniy den'*	Сьогодні сонячний день.
It's dark.	*tem**no***	Темно.
It's bright.	***svee**tlo*	Світло.

What will the weather be like today?
yaka s'ohodnee boode pohoda? — Яка сьогодні буде погода?

What's the forecast for tomorrow?
yakiy prohnoz pohodi na zawtra? — Який прогноз погоди на завтра?

What is the temperature?
yaka temperatoora/skeel'ki s'ohodnee hradooseew tepla? — Яка температура/Скільки сьогодні градусів тепла?
(lit. how many degrees of warmth?)

It's plus/minus ten outside today.
s'ohodnee na voolitsee plyoos/meenoos desyat' — Сьогодні на вулиці плюс/мінус десять.

Is it raining?
chi yde doshch? — Чи йде дощ?

I am...	*menee* ...	Мені ...
hot	*zharko*	жарко
cold	*kholodno*	холодно
warm	*teplo*	тепло

Some Useful Words

black ice	*ozheleditsya*	ожеледиця
downpour	*zliva*	злива
fog	*tooman*	туман
hail	*hrad*	град
ice	*leed*	лід
lightning	*bliskawka*	блискавка
rain	*doshch*	дощ
snow	*sneeh*	сніг
storm	*boorya/nehoda*	буря / негода
thunder	*hreem*	грім
thunderstorm	*hroza*	гроза
cold (n)	*kholod*	холод
degree	*hradoos*	градус
dawn	*sveetanok*	світанок
dusk	*prismerk*	присмерк
sunrise	*skheed sontsya*	схід сонця
sunset	*zakheed sontsya*	захід сонця

USEFUL TIP

You don't have to remember the future tense of verbs. Just use the present tense with the word завтра *(zawtra)* which means 'tomorrow'.

Refer to page 22

Along the Way

Please tell me the way to ...
pokazheet', bood' laska, dorohoo do ... — Покажіть, будь ласка, дорогу до ...

How far is it to the ...?	*chi daleko do ...?*	Чи далеко до ...?
ancient temple	*starovinnoho khramoo*	старовинного храму
beach	*plyazhoo*	пляжу
sea shore	*bereha morya*	берега моря
castle	*zamkoo*	замку
cave	*pecheri*	печери
cemetery	*tsvintarya/ kladovishcha*	цвинтаря / кладовища
forest	*leesoo*	лісу
gorge	*ooshchelini*	ущелини
lake	*ozera*	озера
river	*reeki*	ріки
top/foot of the mountain	*vershini/ peedneezhzhya hori*	вершини / підніжжя гори
spring	*jerela*	джерела
village	*sela*	села
town	*meesta*	міста
tourist base	*toorbazi*	турбази
sanatorium	*sanatoreeyoo*	санаторію
waterfall	*vodospadoo*	водоспаду

How many hours will it take?
skeel'ki hodin tse zayme? — Скільки годин це займе?

Do we still have a long way to go?
*nam shche **dowho** yti?* Нам ще довго йти?

Is it easy to find?
*chi **leh**ko yo**ho**/yee**yee** znay**ti**?* Чи легко його/її знайти?

Are there signs?
*chi tam ye wkazeew**ni**ki/ **zna**ki?* Чи там є вказівники/знаки?

How many kilometres?
***skeel'ki** keelo**met**reew?* Скільки кілометрів?

Directions

Which way?	***koo**di?*	Куди?
By which road?	*ya**ko**yoo doro**ho**yoo?*	Якою дорогою?
In which direction?	*oo ya**ko**moo **na**pryamkoo?*	У якому напрямку?
Left.	*leev**o**rooch*	ліворуч.
Right.	*prav**o**rooch*	Праворуч.
Straight ahead.	***pry**amo*	Прямо.
Back.	*na**zad***	Назад.
Past the village.	*powz se**lo***	Повз село.
Before the village.	***pe**red se**lom***	Перед селом.
To the east.	*na **skheed***	На схід.
To the west.	*na **za**kheed*	На захід.
To the north.	*na **peew**neech*	На північ.
To the south.	*na **peew**den'*	На південь.

Animals

animal	*tva**ri**na*	тварина
wild animal	*zveer*	звір
bear	*ved**meed’***	ведмідь
beaver	*bo**ber***	бобер
bison	*zoobr*	зубр
cat	*keet*	кіт
deer	***o**len’*	олень
dog	*so**ba**ka*	собака
elk	*los’*	лось
fox	*li**si**tsya*	лисиця
hare	*z**a**yets’*	заєць
squirrel	***beel**ka*	білка
wolf	*vowk*	вовк

Birds

bird	*ptakh/* ***ptash**ka*	птах / пташка
crane	*zhoora**vel’***	журавель
crow	*vo**ro**na*	ворона
cuckoo	*zo**zoo**lya*	зозуля
duck	***kach**ka*	качка
finch	*snee**hoor***	снігур
owl	*so**va***	сова
pigeon	***ho**loob*	голуб
seagull	***cha**yka*	чайка
sparrow	*horo**bets’***	горобець
stork	*le**le**ka*	лелека
swan	***le**beed’*	лебідь
tit	*si**ni**tsya*	синиця
woodpecker	***dya**tel*	дятел

Insects & Other Creatures

bee	*bjola*	бджола
insect	*komakha*	комаха
jellyfish	*medooza*	медуза
lizard	*yashcheerka*	ящірка
mosquito	*komar*	комар
snake	*zmeeya*	змія
wasp	*osa*	оса

Plants

birch	*bereza*	береза
branch	*heelka*	гілка
bush	*kooshch*	кущ
bramble	*ozhina*	ожина
camomile	*romashka*	ромашка
carnation	*hvozdika*	гвоздика
chestnut	*kashtan*	каштан
cornflower	*voloshka*	волошка
cranberry bush	*zhoorawlina*	журавлина
fir	*yalina*	ялина
flower	*kveetka*	квітка
gladiolus	*hladioloos*	гладіолус
grass	*trava*	трава
guelder rose	*kalina*	калина
leaf	*listok*	листок
lilac	*boozok*	бузок
lily	*leeleeya*	лілія
lily of the valley	*konvaleeya*	конвалія
linden	*lipa*	липа
narcissus	*nartsis*	нарцис
oak	*doob*	дуб

pine	*sosna*	сосна
poplar	*topolya*	тополя
poppy	*mak*	мак
rose	*troyanda*	троянда
tree	*derevo*	дерево
willow	*verba*	верба

Camping

Camp sites are usually located on the edge of major cities and can be difficult to get to by public transport.

Where is the camping ground?
*de **kem**peenh?* — Де кемпінг?

May I camp here?
***mozh**na toot rozbiti tabeer?* — Можна тут розбити табір?

How much is it per night?
***ya**ka **pla**ta za neech?* — Яка плата за ніч?

Where is the office?
de kontora/admeeneestratseeya/direktseeya? — Де контора/адміністрація/дирекція?

Where are the toilets?
  *de too**al**eti?* — Де туалети?

Can we light a fire?
  *chi **mozh**na roz**kla**sti ba**hat**tya?* — Чи можна розкласти багаття?

Where can I get water?
  *de **mozh**na na**bra**ti vo**di**?* — Де можна набрати води?

Some Useful Words

field	***pol**e*	поле
hut	*fleehel'/boo**di**nok*	флігель / будинок
map	***kar**ta*	карта
refuge	*pri**too**lok*	притулок
rucksack	*ryoog**zak***	рюкзак
sleeping bag	***spal'**niy mee**shok***	спальний мішок
tent	*na**met***	намет
torch	*leekh**ta**rik*	ліхтарик
trail	***stezh**ka*	стежка
well	*kri**ni**tsya*	криниця

Food

Ukrainian cuisine is very varied, and Ukrainians are famed for their hospitality. The food reflects not only the range of national dishes, but also the contact that Ukrainians have had over the centuries with neighbouring peoples. In recent years, international cuisine (especially French and Italian) has begun to make its presence felt and fast-food outlets are beginning to make an appearance.

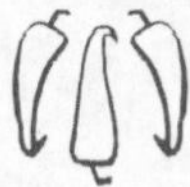

КАСА	CASHIER
ВІДДІЛ	DEPARTMENT/SECTION
ПРОДТОВАРИ	FOOD
ГАСТРОНОМ	FOOD STORE
ОВОЧІ ФРУКТИ	GREENGROCER
БАКАЛІЯ	GROCER
АЗАР / РИНОК	MARKET
КУЛІНАРІЯ	PREPARED FOOD
КОНДИТЕРСЬКА	PATISSERIE
УНІВЕРСАМ	SELF-SERVICE STORE

At the Restaurant

In recent years a number of restaurants, bars and cafes have opened, offering excellent food at reasonable prices with standards of service to match. On menus in Ukraine the adjective describing *how* an item is cooked follows the name of the items itself, eg картопля смажена *(kar**top**lya **sma**zhena)* is literally 'potato fried', балик осетровий *(ba**lyk** ose**tro**viy)* is literally 'fillet sturgeon cured'. The amount of each item that you can expect for your money is still given on some menus, eg 100 г (100 grams) or 1 шт ('one piece').

БАР	BAR
БУФЕТ	BUFFET
КАФЕ (КАВ'ЯРНЯ)	CAFE
ЇДАЛЬНЯ	CAFE/EATING HOUSE
РЕСТОРАН	RESTAURANT
МІСЦЬ НЕМАЄ	RESTAURANT FULL
САМООБСЛУГОВУВАННЯ	SELF SERVICE

Do you have a table for two?
*oo vas ye **sto**lik na dvokh?* — У вас є столик на двох?

Do you have any free tables?
*oo vas ye **veel'**nee **sto**liki?* — У вас є вільні столики?

I want to book a table for tomorrow at six.
*ya **kho**choo za**mo**viti **sto**lik na **zaw**tra na **shos**too **ho**dinoo.* — Я хочу замовити столик на завтра на шосту годину.

Can I/we see the menu?
***mozh**na podi**vi**tisya me**nyoo**?* — Можна подивитися меню?

Do you have a menu in English?
*oo vas ye me**nyoo** anh**lees'**koyoo **mo**voyoo?* — У вас є меню англійською мовою?

What do you recommend?
*shcho vi po**ra**dite?* — Що Ви порадите?

What special dishes do you have?
*ya**kee** oo vas ye fe**er**mo**vee** **stra**vi?* — Які у вас є фірмові страви?

What is this/that?
shcho tse? — Що це?

I would like ...
*ya **boo**doo/veez'**moo** ...* — Я буду / візьму ...
*ya b kho**teew**/kho**tee**la ...* — Я б хотів (m)/ла (f) ...

Can I try that?
***mozh**na pokooshtoo**va**ti ts'**o**ho?* — Можна покуштувати цього?

Could you bring us a good local wine?
*vi **mo**zhete prinesti* | Ви можете принести
***dob**roho mee**sts**evoho vi**na**?* | доброго місцевого вина?

USEFUL TIP

Remember the word for 'Thank you' is дякую (*dyakooyoo*).

The meal was delicious.
*boo**lo** doo**zhe** **smach**no* | Було дуже смачно.

Could we have the bill?
***mozh**na rak**hoo**nok?* | Можна рахунок?

I've been waiting for a long time.
*ya daw**no** che**ka**yoo* | Я давно чекаю.

Please change this glass.
*pomee**nyay**te, bood' **las**ka, **sklyan**koo* | Поміняйте, будь ласка, склянку.

Another place setting please
day**te shche o**din** pri**bor | Дайте ще один прибор

An ashtray, please!
*popeel'**nich**koo, bood' **las**ka* | Попільничку, будь ласка.

Vegetarians

I am a vegetarian.
*ya vehetaree**a**nets'* | Я вегетаріанець. (m)
*ya vehetaree**an**ka* | Я вегетаріанка. (f)

Do you serve vegetarian food?
*oo vas ye vehetareeans'kee **stra**vi?* — У вас є вегетаріанські страви?

I don't eat dairy products.
*ya ne yeem **mo**lochnikh prodook**teew*** — Я не їм молочних продуктів.

I don't eat meat.
*ya ne yeem **mya**sa* — Я не їм м'яса.

I don't eat pork.
*ya ne yeem svi**ni**ni* — Я не їм свинини.

I don't eat fish.
*ya ne yeem **ri**bi* — Я не їм риби.

Eating at a Home

If you are lucky enough to be invited into a Ukrainian home you will be sure of a treat. Ukrainians gladly spend a lot of time and energy in the kitchen preparing food for guests. Virtually everything has to be prepared at home as pre-prepared and frozen foods are not widely available. A traditional festive meal in domestic surroundings begins with a huge number of cold dishes, followed by hot dishes. The aim is to ensure that a guest's plate is never empty. The meal is punctuated by frequent toasts and you will most likely be expected to propose a toast. See page 122 for some toasts in Ukrainian.

Ukrainian Specialities

борщ *(borshch)*
: soup based on beetroot with meat and other vegetables; served with sour cream.

вареники *(vareniki)*
: ravioli-like pasta stuffed with mushrooms, meat, cheese, potato, cabbage, or cherries as a sweet dish.

голубці *(holoob**tsee**)*
: cabbage leaves stuffed with rice and vegetables, or possibly with spiced minced meat and stewed slowly in the oven.

диruни *(diroo**ni**)*
: pancakes made from grated potato and flour and fried; served with sour cream.

холодець *(kholo**dets'**)*
: brawn made by boiling pigs' trotters. The meat is picked off the bone and the gravy sets around it into a jelly as it cools; served with horseradish or mustard.

сало *(**sa**lo)*
: no description of Ukrainian cuisine would be complete without pork fat. Ukrainians like their pigs to be fat for their ***salo***. Spices are rubbed into the skin and the fat is then allowed to stand. It is eaten in thin slices on black bread with garlic and salt and washed down with ice-cold vodka. Especially delicious is the smoked version, копчене салі *(**kop**chene **sa**lo)*.

домашня ковбаса *(do**mash**nya kow**ba**sa)*
: domestic sausage; it is an injustice to call it salami. The only way to sample true home prepared sausage is by experiencing it for yourself with the sights and smells of the markets of Ukraine.

млинці *(mlin**tsee**)*
: pancakes, often made with soured milk for a lighter batter. Thinner pancakes are called налисники *(na**lis**niki)*, which are rolled and served with a stuffing, usually fruit or jam.

Meals

Appetisers

hors d'oeuvres	*zakooski*	закуски
salad	*salat*	салат
meat in jelly	*kholodets'*	холодець
pate	*pashtet*	паштет
assorted cold platter	*asortee*	асорті
fish	*ribne*	рибне
meat	*myasne*	м'ясне
fish/meat in aspic	*zaliwne*	заливне

Soup

Soups form a very important part of the Ukrainian diet. They are often thick enough to be a meal in themselves. Some are served with special buns or breads; you might see з пампушками *(z pampooshkami)* ('with small garlicky buns') written next to a soup on the menu.

first course	*persha strava*	перша страва
soup	*yooshka/soop*	юшка / суп
bean	*kvasolyana/iy*	квасоляна / ий
buckwheat	*hrechana/iy*	гречана / ий
mushroom	*hribna/iy*	грибна / ий
pea	*horokhova/iy*	горохова / ий
potato	*kartoplyana/iy*	картопляна / ий
vegetable	*ovocheva/iy*	овочева / ий
beetroot soup	*borshch*	борщ
bouillon	*bool'yon*	бульйон

Main Course

second course	*drooha strava*	друга страва
beef (cold)	*rostbeef*	ростбіф

beefsteak	*beef**shteks***	біфштекс
beef stroganoff	*bef-**stroh**anov*	беф-строганов
chop	*veedbiw**na***	відбивна
cutlet	*kot**le**ta*	котлета
kebab	*shash**lik***	шашлик
meatballs	*tyoof**tel'**ki*	тюфтельки
meatloaf	*roo**let***	рулет
omelette	*om**let***	омлет
sausage (frankfurter)	*so**sis**ka*	сосиска
saveloy	*sar**del'**ka*	сарделька
schnitzel	***shnit**sel'*	шніцель

Dessert

Dessert in a restaurant is not usually a great affair. The most common item is ice-cream, usually ordered to accompany a cup of coffee or tea. A meal in domestic surroundings is quite another matter. Baking cakes and pies for a festive meal is common in every household. You may also be offered кисіль *(ki**seel'**)*, something resembling drinkable fruit jelly.

cake (large)	*tort*	торт
cake (small)	***tees**techko*	тістечко
ice-cream	*mo**ro**zivo*	морозиво
jelly	*zhe**le***	желе
pie	*pi**reeh***	пиріг

There are different types of jam in Ukraine – варення *(va**ren**nya)* has fruit and is usually too runny to spread on bread; повидло *(po**vid**lo)* is most often made from plums or apples and is also runny; and джем *(jem)* is thicker and can be spread on bread.

honey	*med*	мед
confectionery	*tsoo**ker**ki*	цукерки

Staples

Bread is the staple that is present at every meal. The tasty black bread, made from rye flour, comes in several varieties; the ones to look out for are Український *(ookrayeens'kiy)* and Дарницький *(darnits'kiy)*. A popular form of white bread is батон *(baton)*.

Other staple foods are the various kinds of каша *(kasha)* made from grain. Translating kasha as 'porridge' is misleading, because of the association that the word has with the lumpy grey mass that forms part of the English breakfast cuisine. Buckwheat kasha is an excellent accompaniment to many meat dishes, and can be a vegetarian dish on its own.

bread	*khleeb*	хліб
black	*chorniy*	чорний
white	*beeliy*	білий
breadroll	*boolka*	булка
pasta	*makaroni/ vermeeshel'/ lokshina*	макарони/ вермішель/ локшина
buckwheat	*hrechka*	гречка
rice	*ris*	рис
millet	*pshenichna kroopa*	пшенична крупа
semolina	*manna kroopa*	манна крупа
egg	*yaytse*	яйце
fried egg	*yayechnya*	яєчня

FOOD

Condiments

horseradish	*khreen*	хрін
mayonnaise	*mayo**nez***	майонез
mustard	*heer**chi**tsya*	гірчиця
oil	*o**lee**ya*	олія
pepper	***pe**rets'*	перець
salt	*seel'*	сіль
sauce	***so**-oos*	соус
spices	***spe**tseeyee*	спеції
sugar	***tsoo**kor*	цукор
vinegar	***o**tset*	оцет

Vegetables

aubergine	*bakla**zhan***	баклажан
beetroot	*boo**ryak***	буряк
cabbage	*ka**poo**sta*	капуста
carrot	***mor**kva*	морква
celery	*se**le**ra*	селера
cucumber	*ohee**rok***	огірок
dill	*kreep*	кріп
garlic	*chas**nik***	часник
lettuce	*sa**lat***	салат
marrow	*kaba**chok***	кабачок
mushroom	*hrib*	гриб
onion	*tsi**boo**lya*	цибуля
parsley	*pe**troosh**ka*	петрушка
pepper (sweet)	***pe**rets'*	перець
potato	*kar**to**plya*	картопля
radish	*re**dis***	редис
sweetcorn	*kookoo**roo**dza*	кукурудза
tomato	*pomee**dor***	помідор

Meat

beef *yalovichina* яловичина
chicken *kooryatina/koorka* курятина / курка
duck *kachka* качка
goose *hooska* гуска
ham *shinka* шинка
lamb *baranina* баранина
pork *svinina* свинина
turkey *indik* індик
veal *telyatina* телятина

Seafood

fish *riba* риба
  fresh *sveezha* свіжа
  smoked *kopchena* копчена
carp *korop* короп
caviar *eekra* ікра
  red *chervona* червона
  black *chorna* чорна
cod *treeska* тріска
  cod liver *pecheenka treeski* печінка тріски
crabs *krabi* краби
herring *oseledets'* оселедець

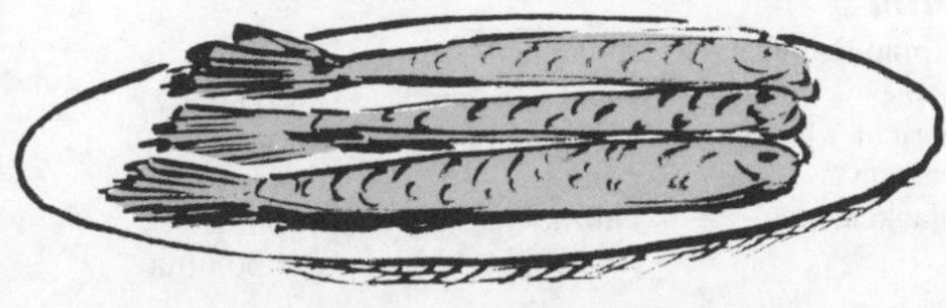

mackerel	***skoom**breeya*	скумбрія
octopus	*kal'**ma**ri*	кальмари
pike	***shchoo**ka*	щука
plaice	***kam**bala*	камбала
prawns	*kre**vet**ki*	креветки
salmon	*lo**sos'***	лосось
sardine	*sar**di**na*	сардина
sprats	***shpro**ti*	шпроти
sturgeon	*oset**ri**na*	осетрина

Dairy Produce

Ukrainians are very fond of milk and dairy products; sour milk in particular for its beneficial effects. Two products have no counterpart in English: кефір *(ke**feer**)* – somewhat like drinking yoghurt, only tastier – and ряжанка *(rya**zhan**ka)* – try it, if you can find it! Butter in Ukraine is always unsalted.

butter	***mas**lo*	масло
cheese	*sir*	сир
cream	*versh**ki***	вершки
margarine	*mar**ha**rin*	маргарин
milk	*molo**ko***	молоко
sour cream	*sme**ta**na*	сметана

Fruit

alpine strawberry	*soo**nit**sya*	суниця
apple	***ya**blooko*	яблуко
apricot	*abri**kos***	абрикос
banana	*ba**nan***	банан
blackcurrant	***chor**na smo**ro**dina*	чорна смородина

cherry (dark, juicy, sweet-sour taste)	***vish**nya*	вишня
cherry (pale, sweet, firm)	*che**resh**nya*	черешня
gooseberry	***a**groos*	аґрус
grapes	*vino**hrad***	виноград
lemon	*li**mon***	лимон
mandarin	*manda**rin***	мандарин
melon	***di**nya*	диня
orange	*apel'**sin**/ poma**ranch***	апельсин/ помаранч
peach	***per**sik*	персик
pear	***hroo**sha*	груша
pineapple	*ana**nas***	ананас
plum	***sli**va*	слива
pomegranate	*hra**nat***	гранат
raspberry	*ma**li**na*	малина
redcurrant	*po**reech**ka*	порічка
strawberry	*poloo**ni**tsya*	полуниця
watermelon	*ka**voon***	кавун

Drinks

Nonalcoholic Drinks

Black coffee is always served in small cups, white coffee in larger ones. Tea is almost always drunk black. If you cannot drink tea without milk, you should ask for it. Tea and coffee is often served with biscuits, cakes and pastries. Tea is often sweetened by jam or honey. You may be served a glass containing a fruit liquid with pieces of fruit floating in it; this is компот ***(kompot)***.

One very refreshing nonalcoholic drink that you may not find on restaurant menus (but will be able to buy on the street) is квас *(kvas)*, made from fermented black bread.

cocoa	*ka**ka**o*	какао
coffee	***ka**va*	кава
instant	*rozh**chin**na*	розчинна
with milk	*z molo**kom***	з молоком
Turkish	*potoo**rets'**ki*	по-турецьки
cappuccino	*kapoo**chee**no*	капучіно
espresso	***ka**va-es**pre**so*	кава-еспресо
iced coffee	***ka**va-hlya**se***	кава-глясе
juice	*seek*	сік
apple	***yab**loochniy*	яблучний
birch	*be**re**zoviy*	березовий
grape	*vino**hrad**niy*	виноградний
orange	*apel'**si**noviy*	апельсиновий
tomato	*to**mat**niy*	томатний
mineral water	*meene**ral'**na vo**da***	мінеральна вода
soft drink	*so**lod**ka vo**da**/ limo**nad***	солодка вода / лимонад
tea	*chay*	чай
with lemon	*z li**mo**nom*	з лимоном
with milk	*z molo**kom***	з молоком
water	*vo**da***	вода

Alcoholic Drinks

Ukraine has a tradition of drinking spirits that goes back centuries. Vodka, or sometimes even cognac, are drunk throughout the course of a meal. Vodka should be drunk 'neat'. There are also vodkas with flavouring. Perhaps the most striking is the one with chilli peppers – pepper flavoured vodka! It is supposed to be a cure for many common ailments. Fruit and alcohol combine to produce an infusion, наливка *(na**li**wka),* that may seem innocuously sweet until you try to stand up; one particularly tasty variety is based on cherries – вишнівка *(vish**nee**wka)*. The wines of Crimea have long enjoyed a world-wide reputation.

beer	***pi**vo*	пиво
cognac	*kon'**yak***	коньяк
liqueur	*lee**ker***	лікер
moonshine	*samo**hon***	самогон
port	*port**veyn***	портвейн
rum	*rom*	ром
sherry	***khe**res*	херес
vodka	*ho**reel**ka*	горілка
Ukrainian	*ookra**yeens**'ka*	українська
pepper-flavoured	*z **per**tsem*	з перцем

wine	*vino*	вино
sparkling	*shampans'ke*	шампанське
dry	*sookhe*	сухе
dessert (sweet)	*desertne*	десертне
red	*chervone*	червоне
table	*stolove*	столове
white	*beele*	біле

Giving a Toast

Toasts are made throughout special meals. Everyone around the table will be expected to propose at least one toast during the meal. (See page 111.)

A word of warning: the small glasses of vodka are supposed to be downed in one gulp when a toast has been proposed. To sip would be regarded as an insult. If you do not think that you will be able to last, it is better to say at the outset that you do not drink alcohol at all. And if you do drink, be especially wary of any

home-produced spirits, самогон *(samohon)*. Needless to say, domestic distilling is illegal, but a lot of people do it and the results – although often better than commercially produced vodka in terms of taste – can be overpowering.

Bon appetit!
*smach**no**ho!* — Смачного!

Cheers!
***bood'**mo!* — Будьмо!

Here's to you!
*za **vas*** — За вас!

Here's to your health!
*za (**va**she) zdo**ro**wya* — За (ваше) здоров'я!

Here's to our hosts!
*za hos**po**dareew* — За господарів!

Here's to the guests!
*za **hos**tey* — За гостей!

Here's to our friends
*za **droo**zeew* — За друзів!

At a birthday party the first toast is always to the person whose birthday is being celebrated: За іменинника (m)/іменинницю (f)! *(za eeme**nin**nika/eeme**nin**nitsyoo!)*. The second toast is always to the parents: За батьків! *(za bat'**keew**)*.

Some Useful Phrases

Thanks, I'm full.
***dya**kooyoo, ya na**yeew**sya /na**yee**lasya* — Дякую, я наївся (m)/ наїлася (f).

FOOD

I don't want to (can't) eat any more.
*ya **beel'**she ne **kho**choo (**mo**zhoo)* — Я більше не хочу (можу).

I don't drink (alcohol).
ya ne pyoo — Я не п'ю.

I'm on a diet.
*ya na d**ee**yetee* — Я на дієті.

The doctor doesn't allow me (to eat/drink that).
*me**nee** ne dozvo**lya**ye **lee**kar* — Мені не дозволяє лікар.

Enough!
***do**sit'!* — Досить!

Some Useful Words

bitter	*heer**kiy***	гіркий
boiled	*va**re**niy*	варений
bottle	***plyash**ka*	пляшка
bottle opener	***shto**por*	штопор
breakfast	*snee**da**nok*	сніданок
broiled (stewed)	*toosh**ko**vaniy*	тушкований
cork	***ko**rok*	корок
course	***stra**va*	страва
first	***per**sha*	перша
second	***droo**ha*	друга
sweet	*so**lod**ka*	солодка
cup	***chash**ka*	чашка
fork	*vi**del**ka*	виделка
fried	***sma**zheniy*	смажений
glass (long drinks)	***sklyan**ka*	склянка
glass (shots)	***char**ka*	чарка

FOOD

glass (wine)	*foo**zher**/**ke**likh*	фужер / келих
hot (spicy)	***hos**triy*	гострий
ice	*leed*	лід
jellied	*zaliw**niy***	заливний
knife	*neezh*	ніж
lunch/dinner	*o**beed***	обід
manager (restaurant)	*admeenee**stra**tor*	адміністратор
marinated	*mari**no**vaniy*	маринований
napkin	*ser**vet**ka*	серветка
plate	*ta**reel**ka*	тарілка
reservation/order	*za**mow**lennya*	замовлення
roast	*pe**che**niy*	печений
salty/salted	*so**lo**niy*	солоний
saucer	***blyood**tse*	блюдце
service	*obsloo**ho**voovannya*	обслуговування
sour	***kis**liy*	кислий
spoon	***lozh**ka*	ложка
supper	*ve**che**rya*	вечеря
sweet	*so**lod**kiy*	солодкий
tablecloth	***ska**terka*	скатерка
waiter	*ofeetsee**ant***	офіціант

Shopping

When prices are given, the word for 'thousands' is often omitted, ie when the taxi driver or the shop owner tells you that you owe them 300 kbv, you of course have to pay 300,000 kbv.

КНИГИ	BOOKS
АПТЕКА	CHEMIST/PHARMACY
УНІВЕРМАГ	DEPARTMENT STORE
ХІМЧИСТКА	DRYCLEANING
ЕЛЕКТРОТОВАРИ	ELECTRICAL GOODS
КВІТИ	FLOWERS
ЗОЛОТО-СРІБЛО	GOLD & SILVER
ПЕРУКАРНЯ	HAIRDRESSER
ПРАЛЬНЯ	LAUNDRY
МАГАЗИН	SHOP
СУВЕНІРИ	SOUVENIRS
СПОРТТОВАРИ	SPORTS GOODS
КАНЦТОВАРИ	STATIONERY
РАДІОТОВАРИ	TV & RADIO
РЕМОНТ ГОДИННИКІВ	WATCH REPAIR

On doors you will see:

ВІД СЕБЕ	PUSH
ДО СЕБЕ	PULL

Buying

I'd like to buy ...
*yab khot**eew**/khot**ee**la **koo**piti ...* — Я б хотів (m)/хотіла (f) купити ...

Where can I buy ...?
*de ya **mo**zhoo **koo**piti ...?* — Де я можу купити ...?

Do you have ...?
oo vas ye ...? — У вас є ...?

Do you sell ...?
*oo vas proda**yet'**sya ...?* — У вас продається ...?

Please show me ...
*pokazh**eet'** (men**ee**), bood' **las**ka ...* — Покажіть (мені), будь ласка ...

How much does it cost?
***skeel'**ki tse (veen/vona) **kosh**tooye?* — Скільки це (він / вона) коштує?

Does it have a guarantee?
*na **n'o**ho/**ne**yee ye har**an**teeya?* — На нього (m)/неї (f) є гарантія?
*veen/**vo**na na har**an**teeyee?* — Він (m)/вона (f) на гарантії?

OK, I'll take it.
*har**azd**, ya ber**oo**/veez'**moo*** — яаразд, я беру / візьму.

I don't like it.
*men**ee** ne podo**ba**yet'sya* — Мені не подобається.

I'm just looking.
*ya **li**she di**wlyoo**sya* — Я лише дивлюся.
I'll have a think.
*ya shche po**doo**mayoo* — Я ще подумаю.

Thanks for your ...	***dya**kooyoo za ...*	Дякую за …
help	*dopo**mo**hoo*	допомогу
advice	*po**ra**doo*	пораду

Can you wrap it please?
*vi **mo**zhete zahor**noo**ti?* — Ви можете загорнути?
How much all together?
***skeel'ki kosh**tooye wse **ra**zom?* — Скільки коштує все разом?

Do you take ...?	*vi priy**ma**yete ...?*	Ви приймаєте …?
credit cards	*kre**dit**nee **kart**ki*	кредитні картки
foreign currency	*eeno**zem**noo val**yoo**too*	іноземну валюту

That's all, thanks.
*tse wse, **dya**kooyoo* — Це все, дякую.

Bargaining

Prices are fixed in state shops (and that means the majority of shops). It might be worth trying to bargain in small privately owned shops at the market.

Really?	***praw**da?*	Правда?
Indeed?	***new**zhe?*	Невже?
You're kidding!	*vi zhar**too**yete!*	Ви жартуєте!

I'm not a millionaire!
  *ya ne meel'yo**ner**!* — Я не мільйонер!
That's too expensive.
  *tse **nad**to do**ro**ho* — Це надто дорого.
Can you make me a better price?
  *vi **mo**zhete zni**zi**ti tsee**noo**?* — Ви можете знизити ціну?
  ***mo**zhna de**shev**she?* — Можна дешевше?
  *a de**shew**she ne **boo**de?* — А дешевше не буде?
I have no/little money.
  *oo **me**ne ne**ma**ye/**ma**lo **hro**shey* — У мене немає / мало грошей.

Souvenirs

You will find painted Easter eggs *(pysanky)* everywhere. Every region has hundreds of distinct patterns, each one with a particular meaning. Embroidery, ceramics and carvings are also popular souvenirs. Don't be tempted by the matryoshki dolls (wooden dolls that fit inside each other) if you are looking for genuine local crafts. There is nothing Ukrainian about them. Antique icons should be avoided, firstly because there is a chance that they have been stolen from abandoned churches during the Soviet period, and secondly because you will need to obtain an export licence to get them out of the country legally.

amber	*boor**shtin***	бурштин
ceramics	*ke**ra**meeka*	кераміка
crockery	*po**sood***	посуд
embroidered ...	*vi**shi**tee ...*	вишиті ...
serviettes	*ser**vet**ki*	серветки
tablecloths	***ska**terki*	скатерки
towels	*roosh**ni**ki*	рушники

embroidered shirt	*vishivanka*	вишиванка
items of wood	*virobi z dereva*	вироби з дерева
jewellery	*prikrasa*	прикраса
necklace (of coral)	*koralee*	коралі
painting	*kartina*	картина

Clothing

ҐУДЗИКИ	BUTTONS
ОДЯГ	CLOTHING
ГАЛАНТЕРЕЯ	HABERDASHERY
КАПЕЛЮХИ	HATS
ПАНЧОХИ / ШКАРПЕТКИ	HOSIERY
ТКАНИНИ	MATERIAL
ВЗУТТЯ	SHOES
РЕМОНТ ВЗУТТЯ	SHOE REPAIR

bra	*byoos**thal'**ter*	бюстгальтер
(woman's) cardigan	***kof**ta*	кофта
dress	***sook**nya/**plat**tya*	сукня / плаття
dressing gown	*kha**lat***	халат
fur coat	***shoo**ba*	шуба
hat	*kape**lyookh***	капелюх
jacket	*zha**ket**/**koort**ka*	жакет / куртка
jeans	***jin**si*	джинси
jumper	***jem**per*	джемпер
nightshirt	*neech**na** so**roch**ka*	нічна сорочка
overalls (or baby's suit)	*kombeene**zon***	комбінезон
overcoat	*pal'**to***	пальто

pants/undershorts	*troo**si***	труси
pyjamas	*pee**zha**ma*	піжама
raincoat	*plashch*	плащ
shirt	*so**roch**ka*	сорочка
shorts	***shor**ti*	шорти
skirt	*speed**nits**ya*	спідниця
socks	*shkar**pet**ki*	шкарпетки
stockings	*pan**cho**khi*	панчохи
suit	*kos**tyoom***	костюм
sweater	*svetr*	светр
swimsuit	*koo**pal'**nik*	купальник
swimming trunks	***plaw**ki*	плавки
tights	*kol**ho**ti*	колготи
trousers	*shta**ni***	штани
underclothes	***nizh**nya bee**liz**na*	нижня білизна

USEFUL TIP

The word не (*ne*) in front of the verb makes the sentence negative.

Refer to page 22

It doesn't suit me.
*me**nee** tse ne pa**soo**ye* — Мені це не пасує

It's not my colour/style.
*tse ne meey **ko**leer/stil'* — Це не мій колір / стиль.

My size is ...
*oo **me**ne **roz**meer ...* — У мене розмір …

Can I try them (it) on?
*mo**zh**na po**mee**ryati?* Можна поміряти?
Do you have a mirror?
*oo vas ye **dzer**kalo?* У вас є дзеркало?
Can I try another size?
*mo**zh**na po**mee**ryati **een**shiy roz**meer**?* Можна поміряти інший розмір?
They don't/It doesn't fit.
*tse ne meey roz**meer*** Це не мій розмір.

Accessories

belt	***po**yas*	пояс
bow tie	***me**telik*	метелик
button	***goo**dzik*	ґудзик
collar	*ko**meer***	комір
cuff	*man**zhet***	манжет
earrings	*se**rezh**ki*	сережки
fastener	*za**stee**bka*	застібка
handkerchief	*no**so**va **khoos**-tochka/nosovi**chok***	носова хус-точка / носовичок
headscarf	***khoos**tka*	хустка
(shoe)lace	*shnoo**rok***	шнурок
necklace	*na**mis**to*	намисто
pocket	*ki**she**nya*	кишеня
ring	***per**sten'*	перстень
scarf	*sharf*	шарф
sleeve	*roo**kaw***	рукав
tie	*kra**vat**ka*	краватка
zipper	***blis**kawka*	блискавка

Footwear

boots	***cho**boti*	чоботи
mules (backless shoes)	*boso**nee**zhki*	босоніжки
sandals	*san**da**lee*	сандалі
shoes	*chere**vi**ki/**too**flee*	черевики / туфлі
slippers	*do**mash**nee **kap**tsee*	домашні капці
trainers	*kro**see**wki*	кросівки

Materials

cardboard	***karton***	картон
cotton	*ba**vow**na*	бавовна
crystal	*krish**tal'***	кришталь
fur	***khoo**tro*	хутро
artificial	*shtooch**ne***	штучне
natural	*natoo**ral'**ne*	натуральне
glass	*sklo*	скло
gold	***zo**loto*	золото
leather	***shkee**ra*	шкіра
linen	*l'on*	льон
paper	***pa**peer*	папір
plastic	*plast**ma**sa*	пластмаса
porcelain	*portse**lya**na/ **far**for*	порцеляна / фарфор
satin	***at**las*	атлас
silk	*showk*	шовк
silver	***sree**blo*	срібло
suede	***zam**sha*	замша
synthetics	*sin**te**tika*	синтетика
velour	***vel**yoor*	велюр
velvet	*vel'**vet**/oksa**mit***	вельвет / оксамит

viscose	*vees**koz**a*	віскоза
wood	***de**revo*	дерево
wool	*sherst'*	шерсть

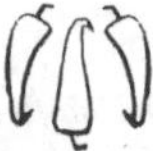

Colours

black	***chor**niy*	чорний
light blue	*bla**kit**niy*	блакитний
dark blue/navy	***si**neey*	синій
brown	*ko**rich**neviy*	коричневий
gold(en)	*zolo**tis**tiy*	золотистий
green	*ze**le**niy*	зелений
grey	***see**riy*	сірий
orange	*zhowtoha**rya**chiy*	жовтогарячий
pink	*ro**zhe**viy*	рожевий
purple	*feeo**le**toviy*	фіолетовий
red	*cher**vo**niy*	червоний
silver	*sree**blyas**tiy*	сріблястий
white	***bee**liy*	білий
yellow	***zhow**tiy*	жовтий

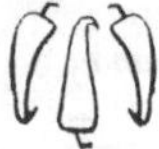

Toiletries

You are more likely to find the items listed below in one of the kiosks that line the streets of the big cities than in a pharmacy.

Can I have ...?	***mozhna/dayte** ...?*	Можна / Дайте ...?

deodorant	*dezodo**rant***	дезодорант
eau de Cologne	*odeko**lon***	одеколон
eau de toilette	*tooa**let**noo **vo**doo*	туалетну воду
eye shadow	*toosh*	туш
face powder	***poo**droo*	пудру
hair lacquer	*lak dlya vo**los**sya*	лак для волосся
handcream	*krem dlya rook*	крем для рук
insect repellant	*reedi**noo** veed **komakh***	рідину від комах
lipstick	*po**ma**doo*	помаду
lotion	*lo**s'yon***	лосьйон
mirror	***dzer**kalo*	дзеркало
nail lacquer	*lak dlya **neekh**teew*	лак для нігтів
packet of tissues	***pach**koo ser**ve**tok*	пачку серветок
perfume	*par**foo**mi*	парфуми
razor	***brit**voo*	бритву
razorblade	***le**zo*	лезо
soap	***mi**lo*	мило
shampoo	*sham**poon'***	шампунь
shaving cream	*krem dlya ho**leen**nya*	крем для гоління
sunblock	*za**khis**niy krem/ krem veed **son**tsya*	захисний крем/ крем від сонця
toilet paper	*tooa**let**niy pa**peer***	туалетний папір
toothbrush	*zoob**noo** **shcheet**koo*	зубну щітку
tube of toothpaste	***tyoo**bik zoob**no**yee **pas**ti*	тюбик зубної пасти

Stationery & Publications

Major Western newspapers can usually be found in the large hotels.

Is there a newsagent nearby?
*chi ye toot neda**le**ko **ha**zetniy kee**osk**?* — Чи є тут недалеко газетний кіоск?

Do you sell ...?	*oo vas proda-**yoot'**sya ...?*	У вас продаються ...?
Do you have ...?	*oo vas ye ...?*	У вас є ...?
newspapers	*hazeti*	газети
magazines	*zhoor**na**li*	журнали
books	***kni**hi*	книги
novels in English	*ro**ma**ni anh**leeys**'koyoo **mo**voyoo*	романи англійською мовою
Ukrainian poetry	*ookra**yeens**'ka poe**zee**ya*	українська поезія
self-teacher of Ukrainian	*samow**chi**tel' ookra**yeens**'koyee **mo**vi*	самовчитель української мови
Ukrainian-English dictionary	*ookra**yeens**'ko-anh**leeys**'kiy slow**nik***	українсько-англійський словник
big/pocket dictionary	*ve**li**kiy/ki**shen'**koviy slow**nik***	великий/кишеньковий словник
guidebook of the town	*poo**teew**nik po **mee**stoo*	путівник по місту
town map	***kar**ta **mee**sta*	карта міста
book on art	***kni**ha z mis**tets**tva*	книга з мистецтва

I need (a/an) ...	***menee** potreeben/ **potreebna** ...*	Мені потрібен (m)/потрібна (f) ...
airmail envelopes	*aveeakon**verti***	авіаконверти
eraser	***hoomka***	гумка
felt-tip pens	*flo**mas**teri*	фломастери
floppy disk	*dis**keta***	дискета
folder	***pap**ka*	папка
notebook	*blok**not***	блокнот
pen	***rooch**ka*	ручка
pencil	*olee**vets'***	олівець
ruler	*lee**neey**ka*	лінійка
writing paper	*pa**peer***	папір

Photography

ФОТОАТЕЛЬЄ	PHOTOGRAPHIC STUDIO
ТЕРМІНОВЕ ФОТО	EXPRESS PHOTO SERVICE

Do you sell film?
*oo vas pro**dayet'sya** foto**pleew**ka?* — У вас продається фотоплівка?

I'd like film with ...	*yab **khoteew**/ **khoteela** ...*	Я б хотів (m)/ хотіла (f) ...
12 exposures	*dva**natsyat'** **kadreew***	12 кадрів
24 exposures	***dvatsyat'** **chotiri** **kadri***	24 кадри
36 exposures	***tritsyat'** **sheest'** **kadreew***	36 кадрів

I'd like film for ...	***menee** potreebna **plee**wka dlya ...*	Мені потрібна плівка для ...
colour prints	*kol'o**ro**vikh foto**zneem**keew*	кольорових фотознімків
colour slides	*kol'o**ro**vikh **slay**deew*	кольорових слайдів

Can you develop this film?
*vi **mo**zhete proya**vi**ti tsyoo foto**plee**wkoo?* — Ви можете проявити цю фотоплівку?

When will the photos be ready?
***ko**li **boo**doot' hoto**vee** foto**zneem**ki?* — Коли будуть готові фотознімки?

Can you develop slides?
*vi proyaw**lya**yete **slay**di?* — Ви проявляєте слайди?

I'd like some reprints.
***menee** potreeb**nee** shche **ko**peeyee* — Мені потрібні ще копії.

My camera is broken.
*meey fotoapa**rat** pola**maw**sya* — Мій фотоапарат поламався.

Can you fix it?
*vi **mo**zhete pola**ho**diti?* — Ви можете полагодити?

Do you sell video-8 cassette tapes?
*vi prodayete **vee**deo-ka**se**ti?* — Ви продаєте відео-касети?

I need some alkaline batteries.
*me**nee** pot**reeb**nee bata**rey**ki* — Мені потрібні батарейки.

camera case	*foot**lyar** dlya/ fotoapa**ra**ta*	футляр для/ фотоапарата
filter	*feel'tr*	фільтр
flash	***spa**lakh*	спалах
light meter	*ekspo**no**metr*	експонометр
wide-angle lens	*shiroko**fo**koosna **leen**za*	широкофокусна лінза

Smoking

НЕ ПАЛИТИ	NO SMOKING

Do you sell tobacco?
*(oo vas) ye w **pro**dazhoo tyoo**tyoon**?* — (У вас) є в продажу тютюн?

A box of matches please.
pro**shoo, ko**rob**koo seerni**keew — Прошу, коробку сірників.

Do you sell lighters?
*oo vas proda**yoot'**sya zapal'**nich**ki?* — У вас продаються запальнички?

Do you smoke?
*vi **pa**lite?* Ви палите?

(Would you like) a cigarette?
*tsi**har**koo?* Цигарку?

Yes, please.
*tak, **pro**shoo* Так, прошу.

No, thanks. I don't smoke.
*nee, **dya**kooyoo. ya ne **pa**lyoo* Ні, дякую. Я не палю.

I'm trying to give up.
*ya nama**ha**yoosya **ki**nooti (**pa**liti)* Я намагаюся кинути (палити).

cigar	*si**ha**ra*	сигара
cigarette	*tsi**har**ka/siha**re**ta*	цигарка / сигарета
filter cigarettes	*tsi**har**ki z **feel'**trom*	цигарки з фільтром
non-filter cigarettes	*tsi**har**ki bez **feel'**troo*	цигарки без фільтру
nicotine	*neeko**tin***	нікотин
pipe	***lyool'**ka*	люлька

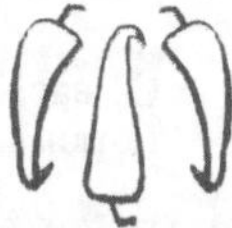

Weights, Measures & Distances

How many kilometres to ...?
***skeel'**ki keelo**me**treew do ...?* Скільки кілометрів до …?

kilometre/s	*keelo**metr**/ keelo**metri***	кілометр / кілометри
metre/s	***metr**/**metri***	метр / метри
centimetre/s	*santi**metr**/ santi**metri***	сантиметр / сантиметри
millimetre/s	*meelee**metr**/ meelee**metri***	міліметр / міліметри
litre/s	***leetr**/**leetri***	літр / літри
half a litre	*peew**leetra***	півлітра
kilogram/s	*keelo**hram**/ keelo**hrami***	кілограм / кілограми
half a kilo	*peewkeelo**hrama***	півкілограма
gram/s	***hram**/**hrami***	грам / грами

USEFUL TIP

It's easy to remember the word це (tse). It means 'This/that is ...' or 'These/those are ...'.

Refer to page 18

Sizes & Comparisons

I want something ...	*ya **khochoo** shchos'...*	Я хочу щось ...
a bit cheaper	***trokhi** de**shew**she*	трохи дешевше
a bit smaller	***trokhi men**she*	трохи менше
a bit larger	***trokhi beel'**she*	трохи більше
of a different colour	***een**shoho **kol'**oroo*	іншого кольору
of a different size	***een**shoho **roz**meeroo*	іншого розміру

big	*velikiy*	великий
small	*malen'kiy*	маленький
long	*dowhiy*	довгий
short	*korotkiy*	короткий
wide/broad	*shirokiy*	широкий
narrow/tight	*vooz'kiy*	вузький
fat	*towstiy*	товстий
thin	*tonkiy*	тонкий
heavy/difficult	*vazhkiy*	важкий
light/easy	*lekhkiy*	легкий
light/bright	*sveetliy*	світлий
dark	*temniy*	темний
a lot/much/many	*bahato*	багато
a little/few	*malo*	мало
more	*beel'she*	більше
less/fewer	*menshe*	менше
too much/too many	*zabahato*	забагато
too little/too few	*zamalo*	замало
some/several	*dekeel'ka*	декілька
a couple	*paroo*	пару
good/fine	*harniy/dobriy*	гарний / добрий
bad	*pohaniy*	поганий
better	*krashchiy*	кращий
worse	*heershiy*	гірший
best	*naykrashchiy*	найкращий
worst	*nayheershiy*	найгірший

Some Useful Words

bag	*soomka*	сумка
box	*korobka*	коробка
briefcase	*portfel'*	портфель

comb	*hrebeenets'*	гребінець
customer	*pokoopets'*	покупець
glasses/spectacles	*okoolyari*	окуляри
gloves	*rookavichki*	рукавички
goods	*tovari*	товари
hairpin	*shpil'ka*	шпилька
handkerchief	*nosovichok*	носовичок
needle	*holka*	голка
pack	*pachka*	пачка
packet	*paket*	пакет
purse	*hamanets'*	гаманець
receipt	*chek*	чек
salesperson	*prodavets'*	продавець
suitcase	*valeeza*	валіза
thread	*nitka*	нитка
towel	*rooshnik*	рушник
umbrella	*parasol'ka*	парасолька

Health

Medical care in Ukraine is free. Western drugs are not easy to find. If you require regular medication, take sufficient supplies with you, together with a note for the customs officials. You should also take any proprietary medicines, eg cough mixtures or headache tablets. Ambulances, швидка допомога *(shvidka dopomoha)*, are a free service and are called by dialling 02.

АПТЕКА	CHEMIST/PHARMACY
АПТЕЧНИЙ КІОСК	PHARMACY KIOSK
РЕЦЕПТУРНИЙ	PRESCRIPTIONS
ПОЛІКЛІНІКА	DOCTORS SURGERY
ТРАВМПУНКТ	EMERGENCY DEPT
МЕДПУНКТ	FIRST AID POINT
ЛІКАРНЯ	HOSPITAL
ПОЛІКЛІНІКА	HEALTH CENTRE
РЕЄСТРАТУРА	REGISTRATION

Complaints

I need a/an ...	*me**nee** pot**ree**ben* ...	мені потрібен …
dentist	*zoob**niy** lee**kar***	зубний лікар
ophthalmologist	*okoo**leest***	окуліст
masseur	*masa**zhist***	масажист

Where is the nearest chemist/ hospital?	
*de nay**blizh**cha ap**te**ka/ lee**kar**nya?*	Де найближча аптека / лікарня?
I feel ill.	
*me**nee** po**ha**no*	Мені погано.
My friend has fallen ill.	
*meey drooh zakhvo**reew***	Мій друг захворів. (m)
***mo**ya **po**droo**ha** zakhvo**ree**la*	Моя подруга захворіла. (f)
Please call a doctor.	
***vi**klichte, bood' **las**ka, **lee**karya.*	Викличте, будь ласка, лікаря.
Is there a doctor here?	
*toot ye **lee**kar?*	Тут є лікар?

I have a pain in the ...	*oo **me**ne bo**lit'** ...*	У мене болить ...
stomach/belly	*zhi**veet***	живіт
ear	***voo**kho*	вухо
head	*ho**lo**va*	голова
liver	*pe**cheen**ka*	печінка
throat	***hor**lo*	горло
tooth	*zoob*	зуб

I feel sick (nauseous).	
*mene **noo**dit'*	Мене нудить.
It hurts here ...	
*oo **me**ne bo**lit'** toot ...*	У мене болить тут.
I've caught a cold.	
*ya zastoo**di**wsya*	Я застудився. (m)
*ya zastoo**di**lasya*	Я застудилася. (f)

HEALTH

I've burned myself.
*ya obpee**ksya*** — Я обпікся. (m)
*ya obpe**kla**sya.* — Я обпеклася. (f)

I have food poisoning.
*oo **me**ne **khar**chove otro**o**yennya* — У мене харчове отруєння.

He/She has been poisoned ...	*oo **nyoho/ne**yee otro**o**yennya ...*	У нього / неї отруєння ...
by medicine	***lee**kami*	ліками
by mushrooms	*hri**bami***	грибами
by tinned food	*kon**ser**vami*	консервами

It's difficult for me ...	***me**nee **vazh**ko ...*	Мені важко ...
to breathe	***di**khati*	дихати
to walk	***kho**diti*	ходити
to swallow	*kow**ta**ti*	ковтати

I can't sleep/walk.
*ya ne **mo**zhoo **spa**ti/khoditi.* — Я не можу спати / ходити.

I've been stung by ...
***me**ne oo**zha**liw/ oo**zha**lila ...* — мене ужалив (m)/ ужалила (f) ...

I've been bitten by ...
***me**ne wkoo**siw**/ wkoo**si**la ...* — мене вкусив (m)/ вкусила (f) ...

The Doctor Might Say

You need ...	*vam neob**khee**dno ...*	Вам необхідно ...
an examination	*zro**bi**ti ob**ste**zhennya*	зробити обстеження

an injection	*zro**bi**ti ee**nyek**tseeyoo*	зробити ін'єкцію
an operation	*zro**bi**ti ope**ra**tseeyoo*	зробити операцію
to submit samples	*z**da**ti **ana**leezi*	здати аналізи
to have your blood pressure taken	*po**meer**yati tisk **kro**vee*	поміряти тиск крові

Take ...	***vi**piyte ...*	Випийте ...
this tablet	*tsyoo tab**let**koo*	цю таблетку
this mixture	*tsyoo meeks**too**roo*	цю мікстуру
this powder	*tsey poro**shok***	цей порошок

You must take it with water.
***tre**ba za**pi**ti vo**do**yoo.* — Треба запити водою.

You must take the medicine three times a day.
*vam **tre**ba priy**ma**ti **lee**ki **tri**chee na den'* — Вам треба приймати ліки тричі на день.

Order this medicine at the chemist.
*za**mow**te tsee **lee**ki w ap**tet**see.* — Замовте ці ліки в аптеці.

Parts of the Body

belly	*zhi**veet***	живіт
blood	*krow*	кров
bone	***keest**ka*	кістка
brain	***mo**zok*	мозок
bronchial tubes	***bron**khi*	бронхи
chest	***hroo**di*	груди (pl)
elbow	***lee**kot'*	лікоть

face	***oblichchya***	обличчя
finger	***palets'***	палець

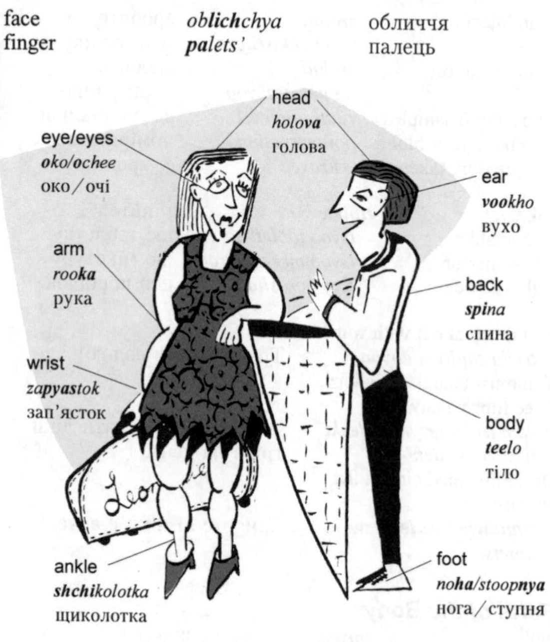

gland	***zaloza***	залоза
gums	***yasna***	ясна
hand	***rooka***	рука
heart	***sertse***	серце
hip	***stehno***	стегно

joint	*soo**hlob***	суглоб
kidney	***nir**ka*	нирка
knee	*ko**lee**no*	коліно
leg	***no**ha*	нога
lip	***hoo**ba*	губа
liver	*pe**cheen**ka*	печінка
lungs	***le**henee*	легені (pl)
mouth	*rot*	рот
muscle	*myaz*	м’яз
neck	***shi**ya*	шия
nose	*nees*	ніс
pancreas	*peedshloon**ko**va za**lo**za*	підшлункова залоза
rib	*re**bro***	ребро
shoulder	*ple**che***	плече
side	*beek*	бік
skin	*sh**kee**ra*	шкіра
spine	*khre**bet***	хребет
stomach	***shloo**nok*	шлунок
throat	***hor**lo*	горло
toe	***pa**lets’ (na nozee)*	палець (на нозі)
tongue	*ya**zik***	язик
tooth	*zoob*	зуб

Some Useful Phrases

I have ...	*oo **me**ne ...*	У мене …
diabetes	*deea**bet***	діабет
epilepsy	*epee**lep**seeya*	епілепсія
high blood pressure	*heeperto**nee**ya*	гіпертонія
rheumatism	*rewma**tizm***	ревматизм

I have an allergy to antibiotics.
*oo **mene** aler**hee**ya na antibee**o**tiki.* — У мене алергія на антибіотики.

I have my own syringe.
*oo **mene** ye **wlas**niy shprits.* — У мене є власний шприц.

My insulin has run out.
*oo **mene** zakeen**chiw**sya eensoo**leen**.* — У мене закінчився інсулін.

I am taking ... tablets/pills.	*ya priy**ma**yoo ... tab**let**ki*	Я приймаю … таблетки.
hormone	*hormo**nal'**nee*	гормональні
contraceptive	*protiza**pleed**nee*	протизаплідні
painkiller	*zne**bo**lyooyoochee*	знеболюючі

At the Optometrist

I need to get my glasses/ lenses fixed.
*me**nee** po**treeb**no po**la**hoditi okoo**lyari**/**leen**zi.* — Мені потрібно полагодити окуляри/лінзи.

I need to order some glasses/ lenses.
*me**nee** po**treeb**no za**mo**viti okoo**lyari**/**leen**zi.* — Мені потрібно замовити окуляри/лінзи.

When will my glasses be ready?
***koli boo**doot' ho**to**vee **moyee** okoo**lya**ri?* — Коли будуть готові мої окуляри?

At the Dentist

I have a toothache.
*oo mene **bolyat'zoo**bi*
У мене болять зуби.

A filling has fallen out.
*oo **mene vi**pala **plom**ba*
У мене випала пломба.

Please give me an anaesthetic.
*zro**beet'**, bood'**las**ka zne**bol**yoovannya*
Зробіть, будь ласка знеболювання.

This tooth has to be taken out.
*tsey zoob **tre**ba **vi**daliti*
Цей зуб треба видалити.

I don't want it extracted.
*ya ne **kho**choo yoho viri**va**ti/vida**lya**ti*
Я не хочу його виривати/видаляти.

HEALTH

At the Chemist

Tampons and condoms are obtainable in the kiosks that line the streets, but check the wrapping and the use-by date before buying.

I need something for ...	
*menee po**tree**bne shchos' veed ...*	Мені потрібне щось від ...
Do I need a prescription for ...?	
*chi me**nee** po**tree**ben re**tsept** dlya ...?*	Чи мені потрібен рецепт для ...?
How many times a day?	
***skeel'**ki ra**zeew** na den'?*	Скільки разів на день?
When will my medicine be ready?	
*ko**li** boo**doot'** hoto**vee** mo**yee** **lee**ki?*	Коли будуть готові мої ліки?

antibiotic	*antibee**o**tik*	антибіотик
antiseptic	*anti**sep**tik*	антисептик
bandage	*bint*	бинт
condom	*prezerva**tiv***	презерватив
contraceptives	*protiza**pleed**nee **za**sobi*	протизаплідні засоби
cotton wool	***va**ta*	вата
cough mixture	*meek**stoo**ra veed **kash**lyoo*	мікстура від кашлю
cream	*krem*	крем
... for the face	*... dlya ob**lich**chya*	... для обличчя
... for the hands	*... dlya rook*	... для рук
shaving ...	*... dlya ho**leen**nya*	... для гоління
nappies	***pam**persi/di**tya**chee peed**hooz**niki*	памперси / дитячі підгузники

painkillers	*zne**bol**yooyoochee*	знеболюючі
plaster (sticking)	***plastir***	пластир
razor blades	***leza***	леза
shampoo	*sham**poon'***	шампунь
soap	***milo***	мило
tampons	*tam**po**ni*	тампони
toothbrush	*zoob**na shcheet**ka*	зубна щітка
toothpaste	*zoob**na pas**ta*	зубна паста
vitamins	*veeta**mee**ni*	вітаміни

Some Useful Words

accident	*nesh**chas**niy **vi**padok*	нещасний випадок
AIDS	*sneed*	СНІД
appendicitis	*apen**dit**sit*	апендицит
asthma	***as**ma*	астма
burn	*o**peek***	опік
cold	*zas**too**da*	застуда
constipation	*za**por***	запор
cough	***ka**shel'*	кашель
diarrhoea	***pro**nos*	пронос
drug addiction	*narko**ma**neeya*	наркоманія
fracture	*pere**lom***	перелом
head cold	*ne**zhit'***	нежить
healthy	*zdo**ro**viy*	здоровий
heart attack	*een**farkt***	інфаркт
haemorrhage	*krovo**te**cha*	кровотеча
high blood pressure	*heeperto**nee**ya/ vi**so**kiy tisk (**kro**vee)*	гіпертонія / високий тиск (крові)
illness	*khvo**ro**ba*	хвороба
indigestion	*ne**traw**lennya **shloon**koo*	нетравлення шлунку

infection	*za**ra**zhennya/*	зараження /
	*een**fek**tseeya*	інфекція
inflammation	*za**pa**lennya*	запалення
influenza	*hrip*	грип
injury	***traw**ma*	травма
low blood pressure	*heepoto**nee**ya*	гіпотонія
menstruation	*menstroo**a**tseeya*	менструація
nausea	*noo**do**ta*	нудота
paralysis	*pa**ra**leech*	параліч
patient	***khvo**riy*	хворий
poisoning	*o**troo**yennya*	отруєння
pregnancy	*va**heet**neest'*	вагітність
pus	*hneey*	гній
sprain	*roz**tyah**nennya*	розтягнення
stomach upset	***roz**lad **shloon**koo*	розлад шлунку
stroke	*een**sool't***	інсульт
swelling	***na**bryak*	набряк
temperature	*tempera**too**ra*	температура
high	*vi**so**ka*	висока
low	*niz'**ka***	низька
thrombosis	*tromb*	тромб
tonsilitis	*an**hee**na*	ангіна
ulcer	***vi**razka*	виразка
veneral disease	*vene**rich**ne*	венеричне
	*za**khvo**ryoovannya*	захворювання
vomit (n)	*blyoo**vo**ta*	блювота
worms	*h**lis**ti*	глисти

Time, Dates & Festivals

Telling the Time

What's the time?
kotra hodina? Котра година?
(lit: which hour?)

The word година *(hodina)*, meaning 'hour', can be omitted in the following list.

one o'clock	*persha hodina* (lit: the first hour)	перша година
two o'clock	*drooha hodina*	друга година
three o'clock	*tretya hodina*	третя година
four o'clock	*chetverta hodina*	четверта година
five o'clock	*pyata hodina*	п'ята година
six o'clock	*shosta hodina*	шоста година
seven o'clock	*s'oma hodina*	сьома година
eight o'clock	*vos'ma hodina*	восьма година
nine o'clock	*devyata hodina*	дев'ята година
ten o'clock	*desyata hodina*	десята година
eleven o'clock	*odinatsyata hodina*	одинадцята година
twelve o'clock	*dvanatsyata hodina*	дванадцята година

To indicate 'half past', Ukrainian inserts the words пів на *(peew na)* before the hour. Instead of saying that it is 'half past' an hour, Ukrainians say that it is 'half into' the next hour. This construction is also used for 'quarter past', чверть на *(chvert' na)*:

half past one	*peew na* ***droo****hoo*	пів на другу
	(lit: half to the second hour)	
half past ten	*peew na odi****na****tsyatoo*	пів на одинадцяту
quarter past two	*chvert' na* ***tre****tyoo*	чверть на третю
	(lit: quarter into the third hour)	
quarter past five	*chvert' na* ***shos****too*	чверть на шосту

In English it is possible to say 'one thirty' as well as 'half past one'. In Ukrainian you can use exactly the same construction:

one thirty	***per****sha* ***trit****syat'*	перша тридцять
	(lit: one thirty)	

The minutes of the first half-hour are constructed in a similar way to 'half past' and 'quarter past':

minute	*khvi****li****na*	хвилина
ten past four	***de****syat' khvi****lin*** *na* ***pya****too*	десять хвилин на п'яту
	(lit: 10 minutes into the fifth hour)	
twenty past seven	***dva****tsyat' khvi****lin*** *na* ***vos'****moo*	двадцять хвилин на восьму

Times from the half-hour to the next full hour have a different structure:

quarter to four	*za chvert' chet**ver**ta*	за чверть четверта
five to seven	*za pyat' khvi**lin** **s'o**ma*	за п'ять хвилин сьома

At What Time?

What time are you leaving?

*o ko**treey** ho**di**nee vi veedlee**ta**yete?* — О котрій годині ви відлітаєте?

(lit: at which hour are you leaving?)

At one o'clock.	*o **per**sheey*	О першій.
At three o'clock.	*o **tre**teey*	О третій.
At eleven o'clock.	*ob odi**na**tsyateey*	Об одинадцятій.

Days of the Week

What day of the week is it today?
***ya**kiy s'ohodnee den' **tizh**nya?* Який сьогодні день тижня?

Monday	*pone**dee**lok*	понеділок
Tuesday	*veew**to**rok*	вівторок
Wednesday	*sere**da***	середа
Thursday	*chet**ver***	четвер
Friday	***pyat**nitsya*	п'ятниця
Saturday	*soo**bo**ta*	субота
Sunday	*ne**dee**lya*	неділя

On what day will you be in Kyiv?
*oo ya**kiy** den' vi **boo**dete w **ki**yevee?* У який день ви будете в Києві?

on Tuesday	*oo veew**to**rok*	у вівторок
on Sunday	*oo ne**dee**lyoo*	у неділю

During the Day

morning	***ra**nok*	ранок
in the morning	*w**ran**tsee*	вранці
in the afternoon	***ooden'***	удень
evening	***ve**cheer*	вечір
in the evening	*oo**ve**cheree*	увечері
night	*neech*	ніч
at night	*oono**chee***	уночі

Months

The names of the months bear no relation to the 'standard' Latin-based words found in so many European languages. The Ukrainian words are much more closely related to natural phenomena, eg February is a 'cruel' month (that is what лютий actually means!). The juice of the birch tree (береза) begins to flow in March – one of the first signs of spring. May is important for grass (трава). In August farmers would get out their sickles (серп) to harvest the grain. The word for November literally means 'leaf-fall', which is somewhat odd, because all the leaves have fallen by the end of October.

month	***meesyats'***	місяць

What month is it?
*yakiy zaraz **meesyats'*** Який зараз місяць?

(in) January	*(oo)* ***seechen'***	січень
February	***lyootiy***	лютий
March	***berezen'***	березень
April	***kveeten'***	квітень
May	***traven'***	травень
June	***cherven'***	червень
July	***lipen'***	липень
August	***serpen'***	серпень
September	***veresen'***	вересень
October	***zhowten'***	жовтень
November	***listopad***	листопад
December	***hrooden'***	грудень

Dates

What's the date today?
yake s'ohodnee chislo? Яке сьогодні число?

It's the fifth.
pyate п'яте.

It's 1 September.
pershe veresnya Перше вересня.

It's 26 February.
dvatsyat' shoste lyootoho Двадцять шосте лютого.

It's 13 July.
tritsyate lipnya Тридцяте липня.

Seasons

seasons	*pori rokoo* (lit: times of the year)	пори року
winter	*zima*	зима
in winter	*wzimkoo*	взимку
spring	*vesna*	весна
in spring	*navesnee*	навесні
summer	*leeto*	літо
in summer	*wleetkoo*	влітку
autumn	*oseen'*	осінь
in autumn	*voseni*	восени

Present

today	*s'ohodnee*	сьогодні
this year	*ts'oho rokoo*	цього року
this month	*ts'oho meesyatsya*	цього місяця
this week	*ts'oho tizhnya*	цього тижня

Past

yesterday	*wchora*	вчора
day before yesterday	*pozawchora*	позавчора
last year	*minooloho rokoo/ toreek*	минулого року / торік
last month	*minooloho meesyatsya*	минулого місяця
last week	*minooloho tizhnya*	минулого тижня

Future

tomorrow	*zawtra*	завтра
day after tomorrow	*peeslyazawtra*	післязавтра
next year	*nastoopnoho rokoo*	наступного року
next month	*nastoopnoho meesyatsya*	наступного місяця
next week	*nastoopnoho tizhnya*	наступного тижня

Regular Events

every hour	*shchohodini*	щогодини
every day	*shchodnya*	щодня
every week	*shchotizhnya*	щотижня
every year	*shchorokoo*	щороку

Useful Words

a year ago	*reek tomoo*	рік тому
always	*zawzhdi*	завжди
at the moment	*teper/zaraz*	тепер / зараз
century	*stoleettya*	століття

during	*peed chas*	під час
earlier/sooner	*ra**nee**she*	раніше
early	***ra**no*	рано
for ever	*na**za**wzhdi*	назавжди
for the time being	***po**ki shcho*	поки що
immediately	*ne**hay**no*	негайно
just now	***teel'**ki-no/**shcho**yno*	тільки-но / щойно
late	***peez**no*	пізно
later	*peez**nee**she*	пізніше
later on/then	***po**teem*	потім
never	*nee**ko**li*	ніколи
not any more	***beel'**she nee*	більше ні
not yet	*shche nee*	ще ні
now	***za**raz*	зараз
since then	*z to**ho** **cha**soo*	з того часу
sometimes	***een**koli*	інколи
soon	*neza**ba**rom*	незабаром
still	*wse shche*	все ще
sundown	*zakheed **son**tsya*	захід сонця
sunrise	*skheed **son**tsya*	схід сонця

National Festivals

Новий рік *(noviy reek)*

The New Year is observed by all. Parties begin on the evening of 31 December and continue throughout the next day. January 1 is a public holiday.

Різдво *(reezdvo)*

Christmas is observed on 7 January, according to the tradition of the Orthodox Church. Carols are sung, and nativity puppet plays are performed.

Старий новий рік *(stariy noviy reek)*
Some families also celebrate the Old New Year on 14 January. They may then go on to take a dip in the (often iced-over) water on the feast of the Epiphany on 19 January.

Пасха *(paskha)*
This is the word used for all the holy days of Easter. It derives from the Hebrew for 'Passover'. Easter is a moveable feast, but it always falls in Spring. The dates of the Orthodox Easter rarely coincide with those of the Catholic festival. Easter Sunday is called Великдень *(velikden')* which literally means 'great day'. Special Easter cakes are baked and brought to church to be blessed. Eggs – real ones, not chocolate – are painted and exchanged as presents. People greet each other with the words Христос воскрес *(khristos voskres)* which means 'Christ is risen'.

День перемоги *(den' peremohi)*
Victory Day – 9 May marks the anniversary of the victory over Nazi Germany in the Second World War.

День незалежності України *(den' nezalezhnostee ookrayeeni)*
Independence Day – a comparatively recent introduction is the celebration on 24 August of Ukrainian independence. These last two festivals are marked by public demonstrations, concerts and special open-air markets; the streets are decorated with flags and banners. Just as with New Year, people send congratulatory cards and telegrams to their friends.

If you are in Ukraine during a major festival (including birthdays) and would like to greet your friends in the Ukrainian way, here are some phrases that may help:

Happy ...	*vee**ta**yoo vas z ...*	Вітаю вас з …
Birthday	*dnem na**ro**jennya*	днем народження
New Year	*no**vim ro**kom*	Новим роком
Christmas	*reez**dvom***	Різдвом
Easter	*veli**kod**nem*	Великоднем

or, more formally:

Accept my congratulations on ...

*priy**meet'** moyee*
*pozdo**row**lennya z ...* — Прийміть мої поздоровлення з …

I wish you ...	*ya ba**zha**yoo vam ...*	Я бажаю Вам …
happiness	***shchas**tya*	щастя
health	*zdo**ro**wya*	здоров'я
success	***oo**speekheew*	успіхів

Numbers & Amounts

Cardinal Numbers

The numbers for 'one' and 'two' change according to the gender of the noun they accompany.

How many?	***skeel'ki?***	скільки?
0	*nool'*	нуль
1	*o**din**/od**na**/od**ne***	один (m)/одна (f)/ одне (neut)
2	*dva/dvee*	два (m & neut)/ дві (f)
3	*tri*	три
4	*cho**ti**ri*	чотири
5	*pyat'*	п'ять
6	*sheest'*	шість
7	*seem*	сім
8	***vee**seem*	вісім
9	***dev**yat'*	дев'ять
10	***de**syat'*	десять
11	*odi**na**tsyat'*	одинадцять
12	*dva**na**tsyat'*	дванадцять
13	*tri**na**tsyat'*	тринадцять
14	*chotir**na**tsyat'*	чотирнадцять
15	*pyat**na**tsyat'*	п'ятнадцять
16	*shees**na**tsyat'*	шістнадцять
17	*seem**na**tsyat'*	сімнадцять

18	*veeseem**na**tsyat'*	вісімнадцять
19	*devyat**na**tsyat'*	дев'ятнадцять
20	***dva**tsyat'*	двадцять
21	***dva**tsyat' o**din**/ od**na**/od**ne***	двадцять один / одна / одне
30	***tri**tsyat'*	тридцять
40	***so**rok*	сорок
50	*pyade**syat***	п'ятдесят
60	*sheesde**syat***	шістдесят
70	*seemde**syat***	сімдесят
80	*veeseemde**syat***	вісімдесят
90	*devya**no**sto*	дев'яносто
100	*sto*	сто
101	*sto o**din***	сто один
200	*d**vee**stee*	двісті
246	*d**vee**stee **so**rok sheest'*	двісті сорок шість
300	***tri**sta*	триста
400	*cho**ti**rista*	чотириста
500	*pyat**sot***	п'ятсот
600	*shees**sot***	шістсот
700	*seem**sot***	сімсот
800	*veeseem**sot***	вісімсот
900	*devyat**sot***	дев'ятсот
1000	***ti**syacha*	тисяча
2000	*dvee **ti**syachee*	дві тисячі
1 million	*meel'**yon***	мільйон
3 million	*tri meel'**yoni***	три мільйони

Ordinal Numbers

Ordinal numerals are adjectives, which means they change form according to the gender of the following noun. Refer to the grammar section (page 14) to check on the different endings. The numerals are given here in the masculine nominative singular.

Which one?	*kot**riy**?*	котрий?
1st	***per**shiy*	перший
2nd	***droo**hiy*	другий
3rd	***tre**teey*	третій
4th	*chet**ver**tiy*	четвертий
5th	***pya**tiy*	п'ятий
6th	***sho**stiy*	шостий
7th	***s'o**miy*	сьомий
8th	***vos**'miy*	восьмий
9th	*de**vya**tiy*	дев'ятий
10th	*de**sya**tiy*	десятий
11th	*odi**na**tsyatiy*	одинадцятий
20th	*dva**tsya**tiy*	двадцятий
21st	***dva**tsyat' **per**shiy*	двадцять перший
30th	*tri**tsya**tiy*	тридцятий

Fractions

¼	***chvert'***	чверть
⅓	*tre**ti**na*	третина
½	*polo**vi**na*	половина
⅔	*dvee tre**ti**ni*	дві третини
¾	*tri **chver**tee*	три чверті

NUMBERS & AMOUNTS

Collective Numerals

Collective numerals are used to count human beings and nouns that have no singular form. Collective numerals above ten are formed by adding -еро *(-ero)* to the ordinary cardinal numeral.

2	***dvoye***	двоє
3	***troye***	троє
4	***chetvero***	четверо
5	***pyatero***	п'ятеро
6	***shestero***	шестеро
7	***semero***	семеро
8	***vos'mero***	восьмеро
9	***devyatero***	дев'ятеро
10	***desyatero***	десятеро

Amounts

How much/many?		
skeel'ki?		скільки?
Could you please give me ...?	***dayte, bood' laska, ...***	Дайте, будь ласка, ...
a bottle	***plyashkoo***	пляшку
a kilo	***keelo/keelohram***	кіло / кілограм
half a kilo	***peewkeela***	півкіла
100 grams	***sto hrameew***	сто грамів
carton	***paket***	пакет
packet	***pachkoo***	пачку
tin/jar	***bankoo***	банку

Some Useful Words

enough	*dosit'*	досить
too much	*zabahato*	забагато
more	*beel'she*	більше
less	*menshe*	менше
many/much/a lot	*bahato*	багато
a little	*trokhi/troshki*	трохи / трошки
too little	*zamalo*	замало
some/several	*keel'ka/dekeel'ka*	кілька / декілька

Vocabulary

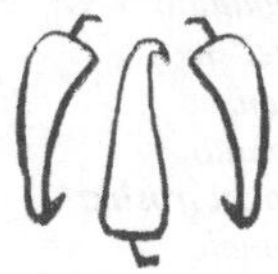

A

able (to be capable)	*mohti*	могти
I can.	*ya **mo**zhoo*	Я можу.
I can't.	*ya ne **mo**zhoo*	Я не можу.
Can you please ...?	*vi ne **mo**zhete ...?*	Ви не можете …?
about/approximately	***bliz'**ko/pri**bliz**no*	близько / приблизно
above (adv)	***vi**shche*	вище
above (prep)	*nad*	над
abroad	*za kor**do**nom*	за кордоном
accept	*priy**ma**ti*	приймати
I accept.	*ya priy**ma**yoo*	я приймаю.
Do you accept?	*vi priy**ma**yete?*	ви приймаєте?
accident	*av**a**reeya/ **neshchas**niy **vi**padok*	аварія / нещасний випадок
accommodation	*zhit**lo***	житло
addict	*nar**ko**man*	наркоман
addiction	*narko**man**eeya*	наркоманія
address	***a**dresa*	адреса

administration	*admeeneestratseeya*	адміністрація
admission (entry)	*(plata za) wkheed*	(плата за) вхід
admission (of guilt)	*viznannya*	визнання
admit (allow entry)	*wpooskati*	впускати
admit (confess)	*viznavati*	визнавати
adventure	*prihoda*	пригода
advice	*porada*	порада
advise	*raditi*	радити
I advise you ...	*ya rajoo vam ...*	Я раджу вам ...
aeroplane	*leetak*	літак
by plane	*leetakom*	літаком
after	*peeslya*	після
again	*znovoo*	знову
against	*proti*	проти
agree, I	*ZHoden*	згоден (m)
	ZHodna	згодна (f)
Do you agree?	*vi ZHodnee?*	Ви згодні?
Agreed!	*domovilisya!*	Домовилися!
agriculture	*seel's'ke hospodarstvo*	сільське господарство
ahead	*wpered*	вперед
aid	*dopomoha*	допомога
airline	*aveealeeneeya*	авіалінія
airmail	*aveeaposhta*	авіапошта
by airmail	*aveeaposhtoyoo*	авіапоштою
alarm clock	*boodil'nik*	будильник
all	*ves'/wsee*	весь / всі
allow	*dozvolyati*	дозволяти
almost	*mayzhe*	майже
alone	*sam*	сам
also	*takozh*	також
alternative (n)	*al'ternativa*	альтернатива

always	_zawzh**di**_	завжди
amazing	_wra**zha**yoochiy_	вражаючий
ambassador	_amba**sa**dor/po**sol**_	амбасадор / посол
among	_**se**red_	серед
ancient	_staro**daw**neey_	стародавній
and	_ee/y/ta_	і / й / та
angry	_roz**hnee**vaniy_	розгніваний
answer (n)	_**veed**poveed'_	відповідь
answer (v)	_veedpovee**da**ti_	відповідати
antique (adj)	_staro**dav**neey_	стародавній
any	_ya**kiys'**_	якийсь
anytime	_koli**ne**bood'_	коли-небудь
appointment	_**zoo**streech_	зустріч
approximately	_pri**bli**zno_	приблизно
archaeological	_arkheolo**heech**niy_	археологічний
argue	_spere**cha**tisya_	сперечатися
argument	_sooper**ech**ka_	суперечка
arrive	_priboo**va**ti_	прибувати
art	_mis**tets**tvo_	мистецтво
ashtray	_popeel'**nich**ka_	попільничка
ask	_pi**ta**ti_	питати
at (place)	_oo/w_	у / в
at (time)	_o/ob_	о / об
automatic	_awtoma**tich**niy_	автоматичний

B

baby	_di**ti**na/nemow**lya**_	дитина / немовля
babysitter	_**nya**nya_	няня
backpack	_ryoog**zak**_	рюкзак
bad	_po**ha**niy_	поганий
bag	_**soom**ka_	сумка
baggage	_ba**hazh**_	багаж

ball (dance)	*bal*	бал
ball (object)	*myach*	м'яч
bank	*bank*	банк
bar	*bar*	бар
battery	*bata**re**ya*	батарея
beach	*plyazh*	пляж
beautiful	***har**niy*	гарний
because	*to**moo** shcho*	тому що
bed	***leezh**ko*	ліжко
bedbugs	*blo**shchi**tsee*	блощиці
before (conjunction)	*persh neezh*	перш ніж
before (prep)	***pe**red*	перед
beggar	*zheb**rak***	жебрак
beginner	*pochat**kee**vets'*	початківець
behind	***zza**doo*	ззаду
below (adv)	*wni**zoo***	внизу
below (prep)	*peed*	під
beside	***ko**lo/**po**rooch z*	коло / поруч з
best	*nay**kra**shchiy*	найкращий
better	***kra**shchiy*	кращий
between (prep)	*meezh*	між
Bible	***bee**bleeya*	біблія
bicycle	*velosi**ped***	велосипед
big	*ve**li**kiy*	великий
bill	*ra**khoo**nok*	рахунок
birthday	*den' na**ro**jennya*	день народження
bitter	*heer**kiy***	гіркий
bless	*blahoslow**lya**ti*	благословляти
blind	*slee**piy***	сліпий
boat	*paro**plaw**/**cho**ven*	пароплав / човен
bomb (n)	***bom**ba*	бомба
book (n)	***kni**ha*	книга

bookshop	*kni**har**nya*	книгарня
bored, I'm	*me**nee** **nood**no/*	мені нудно/
	***nabrid**lo*	набридло
borrow	*pozi**cha**ti*	позичати
May I borrow this?	***mozh**na ya tse*	Можна я це
	*pozi**choo**?*	позичу?
boss	*shef*	шеф
both	*o**bi**dva*	обидва
both (... and ...)	*tak (... yak ee ...)*	так (... як і ...)
bottle	***plyash**ka*	пляшка
bottle opener	*veedkri**vach**ka/*	відкривачка/
	***shto**por*	штопор
box	*ko**rob**ka*	коробка
boy	***khlop**chik*	хлопчик
boyfriend	*drooh*	друг
brave	*kho**rob**riy*	хоробрий
break (n)	*pe**rer**va/*	перерва/
	*veedpo**chi**nok*	відпочинок
break (v)	*la**ma**ti/*	ламати/
	*rozbi**va**ti*	розбивати
breakfast	*snee**da**nok*	сніданок
bribe (n)	*kha**bar***	хабар
bribe (v)	*da**va**ti khaba**rya***	давати хабаря
bridge	*meest*	міст
bright	*yas**kra**viy*	яскравий
bring	*pri**no**siti*	приносити
Can you bring it?	*prine**seet'**,*	принесіть,
	*bood' **las**ka!*	будь ласка!
	(lit: please bring)	
We can bring one.	*prinese**mo***	Принесемо.
	(lit: we will bring)	

VOCABULARY

broken	*rozbitiy/ polamaniy*	розбитий / поламаний
bucket	*veedro*	відро
building	*boodinok*	будинок
burn (v)	*horeeti*	горіти
bus	*awtoboos*	автобус
business	*beeznes/sprava*	бізнес / справа
busy	*zaynyatiy*	зайнятий
but	*ale*	але
buy	*koopoovati*	купувати
Where did you buy this?	*de vi tse koopili?*	Де ви це купили?

C

café	*kafe/kavyarnya*	кафе / кав'ярня
camera	*fotoaparat*	фотоапарат
camp (n)	*tabeer*	табір
camp (v)	*rozbivati tabeer*	розбивати табір
Can we camp here?	*mozhna toot rozbiti tabeer?*	Можна тут розбити табір?
campfire	*bahattya*	багаття
campsite	*kempeenh*	кемпінг
can	*mozhna*	можна
Can I take a photograph?	*mozhna fotohrafoovati?*	Можна фотографувати?
No, you can't.	*nee, ne mozhna.*	Ні, не можна.
can (tin)	*blyashanka/ (konservna) banka*	бляшанка / (консервна) банка
can opener	*veedkrivachka*	відкривачка

candle	_**sveech**ka_	свічка
capital (city)	_sto**lit**sya_	столиця
capitalism	_kapeeta**leezm**_	капіталізм
cards (playing)	_**kar**ti_	карти
care (v)	_toorboo**va**tisya_	турбуватися
I don't care.	_me**nee** bay**doo**zhe/ me**ne** tse ne toor**boo**ye_	Мені байдуже/ Мене це не турбує.
careful	_obe**rezh**niy_	обережний
Careful!	_obe**rezh**no!_	обережно!
carry	_**no**siti/nes**ti**_	носити/нести
I'll carry it.	_ya **boo**doo nes**ti**_	Я буду нести.
cashier	_ka**sir**_	касир
cemetery	_**tsvin**tar/ klado**vi**shche_	цвинтар/ кладовище
certain/sure	_oo**pew**neniy_	упевнений
chair	_stee**lets'**_	стілець
chance	_**mozh**liveest'/shans_	можливість/шанс
by chance	_vipad**ko**vo_	випадково
change (n; money)	_**zda**cha/**resh**ta_	здача/решта
change (n; transport)	_pere**sad**ka_	пересадка
change (v; trains)	_ro**bi**ti pere**sad**koo/ perese**da**ti_	робити пересадку/ пересідати
cheap	_de**she**viy_	дешевий
cheaper	_de**shew**shiy_	дешевший
chemist/pharmacy	_ap**te**ka_	аптека
choose	_vibi**ra**ti_	вибирати
Christmas	_reez**dvo**_	Різдво
cigarettes	_tsi**har**ki_	цигарки
city	_**mee**sto_	місто

city centre	*tsentr **mee**sta*	центр міста
clean (adj)	***chis**tiy*	чистий
close (nearby)	***bliz**'ko*	близько
close (v)	*zachi**nya**ti*	зачиняти
It's closed!	*zachineno!*	зачинено!
cold	*kho**lod**niy*	холодний
come	*ee**ti**/priyti*	іти / прийти
Can we come tomorrow?	***mozh**na **pri**yti **zaw**tra?*	Можна прийти завтра?
Come here!	*ee**deet'** syoo**di**!*	Ідіть сюди!
The bus is coming.	*ee**de** awto**boos***	Іде автобус.
comfortable	*zrooch**niy***	зручний
communism	*komoo**neezm***	комунізм
company (business)	*kom**pa**neeya*	компанія
complex (adj)	*sk**lad**niy*	складний
condom	*prezer**va**tiv/ kontratsep**tiw***	презерватив / контрацептив
Congratulations!	*vi**ta**yoo/moyee pozdo**rov**lennya!*	Вітаю / Мої поздоровлення!
contact lens	*kon**takt**na **leen**za*	контактна лінза
contagious	*za**raz**liviy*	заразливий
contraceptive	*protiza**pleed**niy za**seeb***	протизаплідний засіб
conversation	*roz**mo**va*	розмова
cook (v)	*hotoo**va**ti*	готувати
corner (of a room)	*koo**tok***	куток
corner (of a street)	*reeh*	ріг
at/on the corner	*na **ro**zee*	на розі
corrupt (adj)	*pro**dazh**niy*	продажний
corruption	*ko**roop**tseeya*	корупція
cost (n)	*tsee**na***	ціна

cost (v)	***kosh**toovati*	коштувати
It costs ...	*tse **kosh**tooye ...*	Це коштує ...
How much does ... cost?	***skeel'**ki **kosh**tooye ...?*	Скільки коштує ...?
count	*rakhoo**va**ti*	рахувати
courtyard	*dveer*	двір
crazy	*bozhe**veel'**niy*	божевільний
credit card	*kre**dit**na **kart**ka*	кредитна картка
crop	*ooro**zhay***	урожай
cross (angry)	*roZH**nee**vaniy*	розгніваний
customs (officials)	***mit**nitsya*	митниця
cut (v)	***ree**zati*	різати

D

daily	*shcho**den**niy*	щоденний
damp	*vo**lo**hiy*	вологий
dangerous	*nebez**pech**niy*	небезпечний
dark	***tem**niy*	темний
date (time)	*chis**lo**/**da**ta*	число / дата
dawn	*svee**ta**nok*	світанок
day	*den'*	день
dead	***mert**viy*	мертвий
deaf	*hloo**khiy***	глухий
death	*smert'*	смерть
decide	*vi**ree**shoovati*	вирішувати
decision	***ree**shennya*	рішення
delicious	*smach**niy***	смачний
delightful	*choo**do**viy*	чудовий
democracy	*demo**kra**teeya*	демократія
demonstration (protest)	*demon**stra**tseeya*	демонстрація

depart (leave)	*veedyeezh**ja**ti*	від'їжджати
The flight departs at ...	***vi**leet **rey**soo o ...*	Виліт рейсу о …
What time does it leave?	*o kot**reey** hodi**nee** veed**praw**lennya?*	О котрій годині відправлення?
departure	*veed**praw**lennya*	відправлення
destroy	*rooynoo**va**ti/ **ni**shchiti*	руйнувати / нищити
development	***roz**vitok*	розвиток
dictatorship	*dikta**too**ra*	диктатура
dictionary	*slow**nik***	словник
different	***een**shiy/**ree**zniy*	інший / різний
difficult	*vazh**kiy***	важкий
It's difficult!	***va**zhko!*	важко!
dinner	***obeed***	обід
dirt	*brood*	бруд
dirty	*brood**niy***	брудний
discount	***znizh**ka*	знижка
discrimination	*diskrimee**na**tseeya*	дискримінація
disinfectant	*dezinfee**koo**yoochiy **za**seeb*	дезинфікуючий засіб
distant	*veed**da**leniy*	віддалений
do	***ro**biti*	робити
I'll do it.	*ya tse zrob**lyoo***	Я це зроблю.
Can you do that?	*vi tse **mo**zhete zro**bi**ti?*	Ви це можете зробити?
doctor	***lee**kar*	лікар
dole (unemployment benefits)	*fee**nan**sova dopo**mo**ha bezro**beet**nim*	фінансова допомога безробітним
doll	***lyal'**ka*	лялька
double	***pod**veeyniy*	подвійний
double bed	*dvo**spal'**ne*	двоспальне

	***lee**zhko*	ліжко
double room	***no**mer na dvokh*	номер на двох
down/downstairs	*wniz/wni**zoo***	вниз / внизу
downtown	*tsentr **mee**sta*	центр міста
dream (n)	***mree**ya/son*	мрія / сон
dried	***soo**sheniy*	сушений
drink (n)	*na**peey***	напій
drink (v)	***pi**ti*	пити
I don't drink spirits.	*ya ne pyu spirt**no**ho.*	Я не п'ю спиртного.
Do you drink beer?	*vi **pye**te **pi**vo?*	Ви п'єте пиво?
drinkable (water)	*pit**niy**/dlya **pit**tya*	питний / для пиття
drugs (illegal)	*nar**ko**tiki*	наркотики
drunk (inebriated)	***pya**niy*	п'яний
dry (adj)	***soo**khiy*	сухий
during	*peed chas*	під час
dust	*pil*	пил

E

each	***kozh**niy*	кожний
early	***ran**neey*	ранній
earn	*zaro**blya**ti*	заробляти
earnings	*zaro**bee**tok*	заробіток
Earth	*zem**lya***	Земля
earthquake	*zemle**troos***	землетрус
easy	*lekh**kiy***	легкий
eat	***yee**sti*	їсти
I eat.	*ya yeem*	Я їм.

We are eating.	*mi yee**mo***	ми їмо.
They are eating.	*vo**ni** yee**dyat’***	вони їдять.
economical	*ekono**meech**niy*	економічний
economy	*eko**no**meeya*	економія
education	*os**vee**ta*	освіта
elections	***vi**bori*	вибори
electricity	*e**lek**trika*	електрика
elevator/lift	*leeft*	ліфт
embassy	*po**sol’**stvo*	посольство
employer	*pratse**da**vets’*	працедавець
empty	*po**rozh**neey*	порожній
end (n)	*kee**nets’***	кінець
energy	*e**ner**heeya*	енергія
English	*an**hleeys**’kiy*	англійський
enjoy (oneself)	*o**der**zhoovati*	одержувати
	*zado**vo**lennya*	задоволення
enough	***do**sit’*	досить
enter	*w**kho**diti*	входити
entry	*wkheed*	вхід
equal (adj)	***reew**niy*	рівний
evening	*ve**cheer***	вечір
event	*po**dee**ya*	подія
every	***kozh**niy*	кожний
every day	*shcho**dnya***	щодня
everyone	*wsee/**kozh**niy*	всі / кожний
everything	*wse*	все
exchange (v)	*ob**mee**nyoovati*	обмінювати
exhausted	***zmoo**cheniy*	змучений
exile	*za**slan**nya*	заслання
expensive	*doro**hiy***	дорогий
experience	***do**sveed*	досвід

export (n)	***eks**port*	експорт
export (v)	*vivoziti*	вивозити

F

false	*fal'**shi**viy*	фальшивий
family	*see**mya***	сім'я
fan (cooling)	*venti**lya**tor*	вентилятор
far	*da**le**ko*	далеко
farm	***fer**ma*	ферма
fast (adj)	*shvid**kiy***	швидкий
fast (adv)	***shvid**ko*	швидко
fast (v)	***pos**titi*	постити
fat (adj)	*tow**stiy***	товстий
fat (n)	***sa**lo/zhir*	сало / жир
fault (technical)	*po**shko**jennya*	пошкодження
fault, my	*ya **vi**nen*	Я винен. (m)
	*ya **vin**na*	Я винна. (f)
fear	*strakh*	страх
fee	***pla**ta*	плата
feel	*pochoo**va**ti se**be***	почувати себе
feeling	*pochoot**tya***	почуття
ferry	*po**rom***	пором
festival	*festi**val'***	фестиваль
festival (religious)	*svya**to*	свято
fever	*ha**ryach**ka*	гарячка
few	***ma**lo/neba**ha**to*	мало / небагато
a few	***de**keel'ka*	декілька
fiancé	*nare**che**niy/*	наречений /
	*nare**che**na*	наречена
film (movie)	*feel'm*	фільм
film (roll of)	*foto**plee**wka*	фотоплівка

VOCABULARY

fine (penalty)	*shtraf*	штраф
fire	*po**zhe**zha*	пожежа
firewood	***dro**va*	дрова
flag	***pra**por*	прапор
flashlight (torch)	*kishen'**ko**viy*	кишеньковий
	*leekh**ta**rik*	ліхтарик
flood	***po**veen'*	повінь
floor	*peed**lo**ha*	підлога
on the floor	*na peed**lo**zee*	на підлозі
follow	*ee**ti** slee**dom***	іти слідом
I'll follow you.	*ya pee**doo** za **va**mi*	Я піду за вами.
Follow me!	*ee**deet'** za **mno**yoo!*	Ідіть за мною!
food	***yee**zha*	їжа
food poisoning	*khar**cho**ve*	харчове
	*o**troo**yennya*	отруєння
foreign	*eeno**zem**niy*	іноземний
forever	*na**zawzh**di*	назавжди
forget (v)	*zaboo**va**ti*	забувати
I forgot.	*ya za**boow***	Я забув. (m)
	*ya za**boo**la*	Я забула. (f)
You forgot.	*vi za**boo**li*	Ви забули.
forgive	*viba**cha**ti*	вибачати
formal	*for**mal'**niy*	формальний
fragile	*lam**kiy***	ламкий
free (gratis)	*bezkosh**tow**niy/*	безкоштовний /
	*bez**plat**niy*	безплатний
free (not bound)	***veel'**niy*	вільний
freeze	*mo**ro**ziti*	морозити
fresh	***svee**zhiy*	свіжий
friend	*drooh*	друг
friendly	***droozh**neey*	дружній

full	***pow**niy*	повний
fun	*za**ba**va/**ra**deest'*	забава / радість
funny	***smeesh**niy*	смішний

G

game	*hra*	гра
garbage	*smeet**tya***	сміття
garden	*ho**rod***	город
gas (cooking)	*haz*	газ
gas (petrol)	*ben**zin***	бензин
gate	*vo**ro**ta*	ворота (pl)
generous	***shche**driy*	щедрий
girl	***deew**china*	дівчина
girlfriend	***po**drooha*	подруга
give	*da**va**ti*	давати
Give me ...	***day**te me**nee** ...*	Дайте мені …
I'll give you ...	*ya **dam** vam ...*	Я дам вам …
glass (of water)	***sklyan**ka (**vo**di)*	склянка (води)
glass (of vodka)	***char**ka (ho**reel**ki)*	чарка (горілки)
glasses	*okoo**lya**ri*	окуляри
go (on foot)	*ee**ti**/kho**di**ti*	іти / ходити
go (train/bus/car)	***yee**khati/**yeez**diti*	їхати / їздити
I'm going to ... (do something)	*ya zbi**ra**yoosya ...*	Я збираюся …
I'm going to ... (somewhere)	*ya **yee**doo/y**doo** w/do ...*	Я їду / йду в / до …
Are you going there?	*vi **yee**dete/**y**dete too**di**?*	Ви їдете / йдете туди?
God	*boh*	Бог
good	***dob**riy*	добрий
government	*oo**ryad***	уряд

greedy	*zhadeebniy*	жадібний
grow (eg, 'Trees grow here')	*rosti*	рости
grow (eg, 'I grow flowers')	*viroshchoovati*	вирощувати
guess (v)	*whadati*	вгадати
guide (n)	*heed*	гід
guidebook	*pooteewnik*	путівник
guilty	*vinniy*	винний
guitar	*heetara*	гітара

H

half	*polovina*	половина
handbag	*soomka*	сумка
handicrafts	*remesla*	ремесла
handsome	*wrodliviy/ harniy*	вродливий / гарний
happy	*shchasliviy*	щасливий
hard (difficult)	*vazhkiy/ skladniy*	важкий / складний
hard (not soft)	*tverdiy*	твердий
hate (v)	*nenavideeti*	ненавидіти
have	*mati*	мати
I have ...	*ya mayoo ...*	Я маю …
You have ...	*vi mayete ...*	Ви маєте …
Do you have ...?	*oo vas ye ...?*	У вас є …?
health	*zdorowya*	здоров'я
hear	*chooti*	чути
heat	*speka*	спека
heater	*obeehreevach*	обігрівач
heavy	*tyazhkiy/vazhkiy*	тяжкий / важкий

Hello!	*pri**veet**!*	Привіт!
help (v)	*dopoma**ha**ti*	допомагати
Can I help?	*ya **mo**zhoo (vam) dopomoh**ti**?*	Я можу (вам) допомогти?
Help!	*rya**too**yte!*	Рятуйте!
Help yourself!	*priho**shchay**tesya!*	пригощайтеся!
here	*toot*	тут
high	*vi**so**kiy*	високий
hill	***pa**horb*	пагорб
hire	***bra**ti napro**kat***	брати напрокат
I'd like to hire it.	*ya kho**teew** bi/ kho**tee**lab **wzya**ti tse napro**kat***	Я хотів би (m)/ хотіла (f) бвзяти це напрокат.
holiday (religious)	***svya**to*	свято
holiday (vacation)	*veed**poost**ka*	відпустка
on holiday	*oo veed**poost**see*	у відпустці
holy	*svya**tiy***	святий
home	*deem*	дім
homeland	*bat'keew**shchi**na*	батьківщина
homosexual (adj)	*homoseksoo**al'**niy*	гомосексуальний
homosexual (n)	*homoseksooa**leest***	гомосексуаліст
honest	***ches**niy*	чесний
hope (n)	*na**dee**ya*	надія
hope (v)	*spodee**va**tisya*	сподіватися
hospitality	*hos**tin**neest'*	гостинність
hot	*ha**rya**chiy*	гарячий
hot (weather)	*zhar**kiy***	жаркий
hot (spicy)	***hos**triy*	гострий
hotel	*ho**tel'***	готель
house	*deem/boo**di**nok*	дім / будинок

country house	***kha**ta*	хата
housework	***do**mashnya ro**bo**ta*	домашня робота
how	*yak*	як
How do I get to ...?	*yak do**yee**khati do ...?*	Як доїхати до …?
How are you?	*yak vi se**be** pochoo**va**yete?*	Як ви себе почуваєте?
How much is/are ...?	***skeel'ki kosh**tooye/ kosh**too**yoot' ...?*	Скільки коштує / коштують …?
human (adj)	*lyoo**ds'kiy***	людський
hungry	***ho**lodniy*	голодний
I'm hungry.	*ya **khochoo yee**sti*	Я хочу їсти.
Are you hungry?	*vi **kho**chete **yee**sti?*	Ви хочете їсти?
hurry (v)	*pospee**sha**ti*	поспішати
I'm in a hurry.	*ya pospee**sha**yoo*	Я поспішаю.
hurt (v)	***bo**leeti*	боліти
hypnotism	*heepno**tizm***	гіпнотизм

I

ice	*leed*	лід
with ice	*z **l'o**dom*	з льодом
without ice	*bez **l'o**doo*	без льоду
idea	*ee**de**ya*	ідея
I haven't the slightest idea.	*ya ne **ma**yoo **zhod**noho oo**yaw**lennya*	Я не маю жодного уявлення.
identification	*oosta**no**wlennya **o**sobi*	установлення особи
if	***yak**shcho*	якщо
ill	***khvo**riy*	хворий

VOCABULARY

illegal	*neza**kon**niy/ nele**hal’**niy*	незаконний / нелегальний
imagination	*oo**ya**va*	уява
imitation	*eemee**ta**tseeya*	імітація
immediately	*ne**hay**no*	негайно
import (v)	*oo**vo**ziti*	увозити
import (n)	*wve**zen**nya/**eem**port*	ввезення / імпорт
impossible	*nemozh**li**viy*	неможливий
imprisonment	*oo**vyaz**nennya*	ув’язнення
in	*oo/w*	у / в
included	*w**klyoo**cheno*	включено
inconvenient	*nezrooch**niy***	незручний
industry	*promis**lo**veest’*	промисловість
infection	*za**ra**zhennya/ een**fek**tseeya*	зараження / інфекція
infectious	*za**raz**liviy*	заразливий
informal	*nefor**mal’**niy*	неформальний
information	*eenfor**ma**tseeya*	інформація
injection	*oo**kol**/een**yek**tseeya*	укол / ін’єкція
injury	*po**ra**nennya/ **traw**ma*	поранення / травма
insect repellant	*ree**di**na veed ko**makh***	рідина від комах
inside	*oose**re**dinee*	усередині
insurance	*strakhoo**van**nya*	страхування
insure	*strakhoo**va**ti*	страхувати
It’s insured.	*tse zastra**kho**vano*	Це застраховано.
intelligent	*ro**zoom**niy*	розумний
interested, I’m.	*tse **me**ne tsee**ka**vit’*	Це мене цікавить.
interesting	*tsee**ka**viy*	цікавий

international	*meezhnarodniy*	міжнародний
invite	*zaproshoovati*	запрошувати

J

jail	*vyaznitsya*	в'язниця
jazz	*jaz*	джаз
jeans	*jinsi*	джинси
jewellery	*yooveleernee virobi*	ювелірні вироби
job	*robota*	робота
joke (n)	*zhart*	жарт
I'm joking.	*ya zhartooyoo*	Я жартую.
justice	*spravedliveest'*	справедливість

K

key	*klyooch*	ключ
kill	*oobivati*	убивати
kind	*dobriy*	добрий
king	*korol'*	король
kiss (v)	*tseeloovati*	цілувати
kiss (n)	*potseeloonok*	поцілунок
knapsack	*ryoogzak*	рюкзак
know	*znati*	знати
I know him.	*ya yoho znayoo*	Я його знаю.
know (how to)	*oomeeti*	уміти
I know how to get there.	*ya znayoo, yak toodi deestatisya*	Я знаю, як туди дістатися.

L

lake	*ozero*	озеро

land	***zeml**ya*	земля
landslide	*ssoow*	зсув
language	***mo**va*	мова
last (in a series)	***ostan**neey*	останній
last (eg 'last week')	*mi**noo**liy*	минулий
late	***pee**zneey*	пізній
late, to be	*speez**ni**tisya*	спізнитися
I'm sorry for being late.	***vi**bachte, bood' **las**ka, shcho ya speez**niw**sya/ speez**ni**lasya*	Вибачте, будь ласка, що я спізнився (m)/ спізнилася (f).
I'm late!	*za**peez**nyooyoosya*	Запізнююся!
later	*pee**znee**she*	пізніше
laugh (v)	*smee**ya**tisya*	сміятися
Don't laugh!	*ne **smeey**tesya!*	Не смійтеся!
laundry	*bee**liz**na*	білизна
laundry (place)	***pral'**nya*	пральня
law	***zakon***	закон
lawyer	*advo**kat***	адвокат
lazy	*lee**ni**viy*	лінивий
learn	*oo**chi**ti/viw**cha**ti*	учити / вивчати
I want to learn Ukrainian.	*ya **kho**choo **viw**chiti ookra**yeens**'koo **mo**voo*	Я хочу вивчити українську. мову.
leave (depart)	*veed**kho**diti/ veedyeezh**ja**ti/ veedlee**ta**ti*	відходити / від'їжджати / відлітати
The flight leaves at ...	*lee**tak** veedlee**ta**ye o ...*	Літак відлітає о …
What time does the train leave?	***ko**li veed**kho**dit' **po**yeezd?*	Коли відходить поїзд?

We're leaving for Kyiv tonight.	*oovecheree mi veedyeezhj**a**yemo do k**i**yeva*	Увечері ми від'їжджаємо до Києва.
leave (behind)	*za**boo**ti*	забути
left (not right)	*l**ee**viy*	лівий
legal	*za**kon**niy*	законний
less	***men**she*	менше
letter	*list*	лист
liar	*bre**khoon***	брехун
lice	***vo**shee*	воші
life	*zhit**tya***	життя
lift/elevator	*leeft*	ліфт
light (adj)	*lekh**kiy***	легкий
light (n)	***svee**tlo*	світло
lighter (n)	*zapal'**nich**ka*	запальничка
like (similar)	***skho**zhiy*	схожий
like (v)	*po**do**batisya*	подобатися
I like ...	*nam po**do**bayet'sya ...*	Нам подобається ...
Do you like ...?	*vam po**do**bayet'sya ...?*	Вам подобається ...?
line	***lee**neeya*	лінія
listen	***sloo**khati*	слухати
Listen to me!	*pos**loo**khayte me**ne**!*	Послухайте мене!
little	***ma**len'kiy*	маленький
little (quantity)	***ma**lo*	мало
live	*zhi**ti***	жити
I live in ...	*ya zhi**voo** w ...*	Я живу в ...
Where do you live?	*de vi zhi**ve**te?*	Де ви живете?
lock (n)	*za**mok***	замок

long	*dow**hi**y*	довгий
long ago	*daw**no***	давно
look for	*shoo**ka**ti*	шукати
lose	*zahoo**bi**ti*	загубити
I've lost my money.	*ya **hro**shee zahoo**biw**/ zahoo**bi**la*	Я гроші загубив (m)/ загубила (f).
lose (one's way)	*zablоо**ka**ti*	заблукати
I'm lost.	*ya zabloo**kaw***	Я заблукав. (m)
	*ya zabloo**ka**la*	Я заблукала. (f)
lost (adj)	*w**tra**cheniy*	втрачений
loud	*holos**niy***	голосний
love (n)	*lyoo**bow**/ko**khan**nya*	любов / кохання
love (be fond of)	*lyoo**bi**ti*	любити
I'm fond of ...	*ya **doo**zhe lyoob**lyoo** ...*	Я дуже люблю …
Are you fond of ...?	*vi **lyoo**bite ...?*	Ви любите …?
love (relationships)	*ko**kha**ti*	кохати
I love you.	*ya te**be** ko**kha**yoo*	Я тебе кохаю.
lucky	*shchas**li**viy*	щасливий
lucky, to be	***ma**ti **shchas**tya* (lit: to have luck)	мати щастя
lunch	*o**beed***	обід

M

machine	*ma**shi**na*	машина
mad (crazy)	*bozhe**veel'**niy*	божевільний
made of	*(**zro**bleniy) z*	(зроблений) з
majority	***beel'**sheest'*	більшість
make	*zro**bi**ti*	зробити
Did you make it?	*vi **sa**mee tse*	Ви самі це

	*zro**bi**li?*	зробили?
many	***ba**hato* → *ba**ha**to*	багато
map	***kar**ta*	карта
market	***ri**nok*	ринок
at the market	*na **rin**koo*	на ринку
marriage	*odroo**zhen**nya*	одруження
marry		
(man to a woman)	*odroo**zhi**tisya*	одружитися
(woman to a man)	***viy**ti za**meezh***	вийти заміж
I got married.	*ya odroo**zhiw**sya*	Я одружився.
	*ya **viy**shla za**meezh***	Я вийшла заміж.
massage	*ma**sazh***	масаж
matches	***seer**niki*	сірники
maybe	***ma**boot'*	мабуть
meet (someone)	*zoo**stree**ti*	зустріти
I'll meet you.	*ya vas zoo**stree**noo*	Я вас зустріну.
meet (each other)	*zoo**stree**tisya*	зустрітися
Let's meet!	*zoo**streen'**mosya!*	зустріньмося!
menu	*me**nyoo***	меню
message	*povee**dom**lennya*	повідомлення
mind (n)	***ro**zoom*	розум
mind (to object)	*zape**re**choovati*	заперечувати
Do you mind ...?	***mozh**na me**nee** ...?*	Можна мені…?
	*vi ne zape**re**chooyete?*	Ви не заперечуєте?
Never mind!	*nee**cho**ho!*	нічого!
Mind out!	*obe**rezh**no!*	обережно!
minute	*khvi**li**na*	хвилина
miss, I	*soo**moo**yoo za ...*	сумую за …
mistake	*po**mil**ka*	помилка
mistake, to make a	*pomi**li**tisya*	помилитися

You've made a mistake.	*vi pomililisya*	ви помилилися.
mix	*zmeeshoovati*	змішувати
modern	*soochasniy*	сучасний
money	*hroshee*	гроші
monument	*pamyatnik*	пам'ятник
more	*beel'she*	більше
morning	*ranok*	ранок
mountain	*hora*	гора
mountaineering	*al'peeneezm*	альпінізм
movie	*feel'm*	фільм
Let's see a movie.	*khodeemo do keeno*	Ходімо до кіно.
museum	*moozey*	музей
music	*moozika*	музика

N

name	*eemya*	ім'я
My name is ...	*moye eemya ...*	Моє ім'я …
	mene zvoot'...	Мене звуть …
	(lit: they call me)	
What's your name?	*yak vashe eemya?*	Як ваше ім'я?
	yak vas zvoot'?	Як вас звуть?
	(lit: how do they call you?)	
national park	*zapoveednik*	заповідник
nature	*priroda*	природа
near (adv)	*bliz'ko*	близько
near (prep)	*beelya*	біля
nearby	*porooch*	поруч
necessary	*potreebniy*	потрібний
need	*treba/potreebno*	треба / потрібно

I need ...	*me**nee** **tre**ba/* *po**tree**bno ...*	мені треба/ потрібно ...
We need ...	*nam **tre**ba/* *po**tree**bno ...*	нам треба/ потрібно ...
Do you need anything?	*vam shchos'* ***tre**ba/* *po**tree**bno?*	Вам щось треба/ потрібно?
neither	*nee*	ні
never	*nee**ko**li*	ніколи
new	*no**viy***	новий
news	*novi**na**/no**vi**ni*	новина (sg) новини (pl)
newspaper	*ha**ze**ta*	газета
next	*na**stoop**niy*	наступний
night	*neech*	ніч
No.	*nee*	Ні.
noise	*shoom*	шум
noisy	***shoom**niy*	шумний
none	***zhod**niy*	жодний
There isn't a single ...	*ne**ma**ye* ***zhod**noho ...*	немає жодного ...
Not any more.	***beel'**she nee*	Більше ні.
I don't smoke any more.	*ya **beel'**she ne* *koor**yoo***	Я більше не курю.
nothing	*nee**shcho**/nee**cho**ho*	ніщо/нічого
not yet.	*shche nee*	Ще ні.
We aren't in L'viv yet.	*mi shche ne oo* ***l'vo**vee.*	Ми ще не у Львові.
now	*te**per**/za**raz***	тепер/зараз
nuclear energy	***a**tomna e**ner**heeya*	атомна енергія

VOCABULARY

O

obvious	*oche**vid**niy*	очевидний
occupation	*za**nya**ttya*	заняття
ocean	*o**kean***	океан
offend	*obra**zha**ti*	ображати
offer (v)	*propono**va**ti*	пропонувати
office	*kon**to**ra/byoo**ro***	контора / бюро
often	***chas**to*	часто
oil	***naf**ta*	нафта
oil (cooking)	*o**lee**ya*	олія
old	*sta**riy***	старий
on (location)	*na*	на
on (a particular day)	*oo/w*	у / в
once	*raz*	раз
once more	*shche raz*	ще раз
once (upon a time)	***ko**lis'*	колись
one	*o**din***	один
only	***teel'**ki*	тільки
open (adj)		
(doors, windows)	*veed**chi**neniy*	відчинений
(shop)	*veed**kri**tiy*	відкритий
open (v)		
(doors, windows)	*veedchi**nya**ti*	відчиняти
(shop)	*veedkri**va**ti*	відкривати
opinion	***doom**ka*	думка
in my opinion	*na moyoo **doom**koo*	на мою думку
opportunity	*na**ho**da*	нагода
opposite (adj)	*proti**lezh**niy*	протилежний
opposite (prep)	*na**pro**ti*	напроти
or	*a**bo**/chi*	або / чи
order (command)	*na**kaz***	наказ

VOCABULARY

order (something)	*zamowlennya*	замовлення
order (v)	*zamoviti*	замовити
ordinary	*zvichayniy*	звичайний
organisation	*orhaneezatseeya*	організація
organise (v)	*vlashtovoovati*	влаштовувати
original	*oriheenal'niy*	оригінальний
other	*eenshiy*	інший
outside	*nazownee*	назовні
over (prep)	*nad*	над
overnight (v)	*perenochoovati*	переночувати
overseas	*za kordonom*	за кордоном
owe	*zaviniti/ booti vinnim*	завинити / бути винним
I owe you.	*ya vam vinen*	Я Вам винен.
You owe me.	*vi menee vinnee*	Ви мені винні.
owner	*wlasnik*	власник

P

pack (of cigarettes)	*pachka (tsiharok)*	пачка (цигарок)
package	*pakoonok*	пакунок
packet	*paket*	пакет
padlock	*visyachiy zamok*	висячий замок
painful	*bolyoochiy*	болючий
pair	*para*	пара
paper	*papeer*	папір
parcel	*posilka*	посилка
park	*park*	парк
parliament	*parlament*	парламент
part	*chastka/chastina*	частка / частина
participate	*brati oochast'*	брати участь
participation	*oochast'*	участь

party	*ve**cheer**ka*	вечірка
party (political)	***par**teeya*	партія
passenger	*pasa**zhir***	пасажир
passport	***pas**port*	паспорт
path	***stezh**ka*	стежка
pay (v)	*pla**ti**ti*	платити
peace	***mir***	мир
people (crowd)	***lyoo**di*	люди
lots of people	*ba**ha**to **lyoo**dey*	багато людей
people (nation)	*na**rod***	народ
perfect (adj)	*dosko**na**liy*	досконалий
permanent	*pos**teey**niy*	постійний
permission	*doz**veel***	дозвіл
with your permission	*z **va**shoho doz**vo**loo*	з Вашого дозволу
permit (n)	*pere**poos**tka*	перепустка
permit (v)	*dozvo**lya**ti*	дозволяти
persecution	*peres**lee**doovannya*	переслідування
person	*o**so**ba*	особа
personal	*oso**bis**tiy*	особистий
personality	*oso**bis**teest'*	особистість
pharmacy	*ap**te**ka*	аптека
photograph (n)	*foto**hra**feeya*	фотографія
photograph (v)	*fotohrafoo**va**ti*	фотографувати
Can I take a photograph?	*chi **mozh**na fotohrafoo**va**ti?*	Чи можна фотографувати?
piece	*shma**tok***	шматок
place (n)	***mees**tse*	місце
plant (n)	*ros**li**na*	рослина
play (n) (theatrical)	*pyesa/vistava*	п'єса / вистава
play (v)	*hra**ti***	грати

VOCABULARY

Please.	*bood' **laska***	Будь ласка.
plenty	***ba**hato*	багато
point (v)	*poka**zoo**vati*	показувати
	***(pal'**tsem)*	(пальцем)
police	*mee**lee**tseeya*	міліція
politics	*po**lee**tika*	політика
pollution	*za**brood**nennya*	забруднення
pool (swimming)	*ba**seyn***	басейн
poor	***beed**niy*	бідний
positive (certain)	*oo**pew**neniy*	упевнений
I'm positive.	*ya **pe**ven/**pew**na*	Я певен. (m)
		Я певна. (f)
postcard	*lis**tee**wka*	листівка
pottery (items)	*fa**yans**/kera**mee**ka*	фаянс / кераміка
pottery (place)	*hon**char**nya*	гончарня
poverty	***beed**neest'*	бідність
power (strength)	***si**la*	сила
power (political)	*w**la**da*	влада
practical	*prak**tich**niy*	практичний
prayer	*mo**lit**va*	молитва
prefer	*na**da**vati pere**va**hoo*	надавати перевагу
I prefer ...	*ya nada**yoo***	Я надаю
	*pere**va**hoo ...*	перевагу ...
pregnant	*va**heet**na*	вагітна
present (adj)	*te**pe**reeshneey/*	теперішній /
	***ni**neeshneey*	нинішний
present (gift)	*poda**roo**nok*	подарунок
president	*prezi**dent***	президент
pretty	***har**niy*	гарний
prevent	*pereshko**ja**ti/*	перешкоджати /
	*zapo**bee**hati*	запобігати
price	***tsee**na*	ціна

VOCABULARY

priest	*svyashchennik*	священник
prime minister	*premyer ministr*	прем'єр міністр
prison	*vyaznitsya*	в'язниця
prisoner	*vyazen'*	в'язень (m & f)
private	*privatniy*	приватний
probably	*ymoveerno*	ймовірно
problem	*problema*	проблема
procession	*protseseeya*	процесія
produce (v)	*viroblyati*	виробляти
professional	*profeseeyniy*	професійний
profit	*pribootok*	прибуток
promise (n)	*obeetsyanka*	обіцянка
promise (v)	*obeetsyati*	обіцяти
prostitute	*prostitootka*	проститутка
protect	*zakhishchati*	захищати
protest (n)	*protest*	протест
protest (v)	*protestoovati*	протестувати
public (n)	*poobleeka*	публіка
public (adj)	*poobleechniy/ hromads'kiy*	публічний / громадський
in public	*poobleechno*	публічно
pull	*tyahti*	тягти
push	*shtowkhati*	штовхати

Q

quality	*yakeest'*	якість
of good quality	*yakeesniy*	якісний
question (n)	*pitannya*	питання
quick (adj)	*shvidkiy*	швидкий
quickly	*shvidko*	швидко
quiet (adj)	*spokeeyniy/tikhiy*	спокійний / тихий

R

race (contest)	*beeh*	біг
race (horses)	***skach**ki/pere**ho**ni*	скачки / перегони
racist	*ra**sist***	расист
radio	***ra**deeo*	радіо
railway	*za**leez**nitsya*	залізниця
by railway	*za**leez**nitseyoo*	залізницею
rain	*doshch*	дощ
It's raining.	***ee**de doshch*	іде дощ.
rape (n)	*ZHvaltoo**van**nya*	згвалтування
rape (v)	*hvaltoo**va**ti*	гвалтувати
rare (unusual)	***reed**keesniy*	рідкісний
rare (meat)	*nedos**ma**zheniy*	недосмажений
raw	*si**riy***	сирий
ready	*ho**to**viy*	готовий
reason (n)	*pri**chi**na*	причина
receipt	*kvi**tan**tseeya*	квитанція
recently	*neshcho**daw**no*	нещодавно
recommend	*rekomendoo**va**ti*	рекомендувати
refugee	***bee**zhenets'*	біженець
refund (n)	***vi**plata/ veedshkodoo**van**nya*	виплата / відшкодування
refuse (n)	***smeet**tya*	сміття
refuse (v)	*veedmow**lya**tisya*	відмовлятися
region	*ra**yon***	район
regulation	***pra**vilo*	правило
relationship	*sto**soon**ki*	стосунки
relax	*rosslab**lya**tisya*	розслаблятися
religion	*re**lee**heeya*	релігія
remember	*pam**ya**tati*	пам'ятати
remote	*veed**da**leniy*	віддалений

VOCABULARY

rent (n; accomm)	*kvar**tir**na **pla**ta*	квартирна плата
rent (n; hiring)	*pro**kat**/o**ren**da*	прокат / оренда
rent (v)	*nay**ma**ti*	наймати
representative	*predstaw**nik***	представник
republic	*res**poob**leeka*	республіка
reservation	*(pope**red**nye) za**mow**lennya*	(попереднє) замовлення
reserve (n)	*zapo**veed**nik*	заповідник
reserve (v)	*zamow**lya**ti*	замовляти
respect (n)	*po**va**ha*	повага
respect (v)	*shanoo**va**ti*	шанувати
responsibility	*veedpovee**dal'**neest'*	відповідальність
rest (n)	*veedpo**chi**nok*	відпочинок
rest (v)	*veedpochi**va**ti*	відпочивати
restaurant	*resto**ran***	ресторан
return	*pover**ta**tisya*	повертатися
We'll return on ...	*mi pover**ta**yemosya ...*	Ми повертаємося ...
return ticket	*zvo**rot**niy kvi**tok***	зворотний квиток
revolution	*revo**lyoo**tseeya*	революція
rich	*ba**ha**tiy*	багатий
right (not left)	***pra**viy*	правий
on the right	*pravo**rooch***	праворуч
right, I'm	*ya **ma**yoo **ra**tseeyoo*	Я маю рацію.
risk	*rizik*	ризик
road	*do**ro**ha*	дорога
robber	*hra**beezh**nik*	грабіжник
robbery	*pohrab*	пограб
roof	*dakh*	дах
room	*keem**na**ta*	кімната
room (hotel)	***no**mer*	номер
rope	*ka**nat***	канат

VOCABULARY

round	*__krooh__liy*	круглий
rubbish	*__smeet__tya*	сміття
ruins	*roo__yee__ni*	руїни
rule	*__pra__vilo*	правило

S

sad	*soom__niy__*	сумний
safe (adj)	*nepo__shko__jeniy*	непошкоджений
safe (n)	*seyf*	сейф
safety	*bez__pe__ka*	безпека
salty	*so__lo__niy*	солоний
same	*toy __sa__miy*	той самий
say	*hovo__ri__ti/ska__za__ti*	говорити / сказати
I said ...	*ya ska__zaw__ ...*	Я сказав ... (m)
	ya ska__za__la ...	Я сказала ... (f)
Can you say that again?	*powto__reet'__, bood' __las__ka.* (lit: repeat, please)	Повторіть, будь ласка.
scenery	*pey__zazh__*	пейзаж
secret (adj)	*ta__yem__niy*	таємний
secret (n)	*tayem__ni__tsya*	таємниця
see	*__ba__chiti*	бачити
I see. (understand)	*ya rozoo__mee__yoo.*	Я розумію.
I see (it).	*ya __ba__choo (tse)*	Я бачу (це).
selfish	*ehoyees__ti__chniy*	егоїстичний
sell	*proda__va__ti*	продавати
Do you sell ...?	*vi proda__ye__te ...?*	Ви продаєте ...?
send	*posi__la__ti*	посилати
serious	*se__ryoz__niy*	серйозний
several	*__keel'__ka/de__keel'__ka*	кілька / декілька

shade	*teen'*	тінь
share (n)	***chast**ka*	частка
share (v)	*rozdee**lya**ti*	розділяти
shop	*kram**ni**tsya/*	крамниця /
	*maha**zin***	магазин
short (time)	*ne**dow**hiy*	недовгий
a short time ago	*ne**daw**no*	недавно
short (height)	*ko**rot**kiy*	короткий
shortage	*nedo**sta**cha*	недостача
shout	*kri**cha**ti*	кричати
show (v)	*po**ka**zoovati*	показувати
Show me, please.	*poka**zheet'**,*	Покажіть,
	*bood' **las**ka.*	будь ласка.
shut (adj)	*za**chi**neniy*	зачинений
shut (v)	*zachi**nya**ti*	зачиняти
shy	*boyaz**kiy***	боязкий
sick	***khvo**riy*	хворий
sickness	*khvo**ro**ba*	хвороба
sign	*znak*	знак
similar	*po**deeb**niy*	подібний
since (from that time)	*z **to**ho **cha**soo*	з того часу
since (because)	*os**keel'**ki*	оскільки
since (after that time)	*z **to**ho **cha**soo yak ...*	з того часу як …
since (prep)	*z, **pees**lya*	з, після
single (unmarried)	*neo**droo**zheniy/*	неодружений (m)/
	*neza**meezh**nya*	незаміжня (f)
sit	*see**da**ti*	сідати
Sit down!	*see**day**te!*	сідайте!
sit (be sitting)	*si**dee**ti*	сидіти
situation	*sitooat**see**ya*	ситуація

size	*rozmeer*	розмір
sleep (n)	*son*	сон
sleep (v)	*spati*	спати
I'm asleep.	*ya splyoo*	Я сплю.
He is asleep.	*veen spit'*	Він спить.
Are you asleep?	*vi spite?*	Ви спите?
sleepy	*sonniy*	сонний
I'm sleepy.	*ya khochoo spati.*	Я хочу спати.
slow	*poveel'niy*	повільний
slowly	*poveel'no*	повільно
small	*maliy*	малий
smell (n)	*zapakh*	запах
smell (v)	*veedchoovati zapakh*	відчувати запах
socialism	*sotseealeezm*	соціалізм
solid (adj)	*sootseel'niy*	суцільний
some (quantity)	*keel'ka/dekeel'ka*	кілька / декілька
somebody	*khtos'*	хтось
something	*shchos'*	щось
sometimes	*eenkoli*	інколи
song	*speew*	спів
soon	*nezabarom*	незабаром
sorry, I'm	*vibachte!*	Вибачте!
souvenir	*sooveneer*	сувенір
special	*spetseeal'niy*	спеціальний
spirits	*spirtnee napoyee*	спиртні напої
sport	*sport*	спорт
standard (adj)	*standartniy*	стандартний
stay (n)	*pereboovannya*	перебування
stay (v)	*probooti*	пробути
I shall stay here for two days.	*ya proboodoo toot dva dnee.*	Я пробуду тут два дні.
steal	*krasti*	красти

My money has been stolen.	*oo **me**ne **wkra**deno **hro**shee.*	У мене вкрадено гроші.
stop (n)	*zoo**pin**ka*	зупинка
stop (v)	*zoopi**ni**ti*	зупинити
I stopped the car.	*ya zoopi**niw**/ zoopi**ni**la ma**shi**noo*	Я зупинив (m)/ зупинила (f) машину.
stop (v)	*zoopi**ni**tisya*	зупинитися
The car stopped.	*ma**shi**na zoopi**ni**lasya.*	Машина зупинилася.
storey	***po**verkh*	поверх
on the ground floor	*na **per**shomoo **po**versee* (lit: on the 1st floor)	на першому поверсі
storm	***boo**rya/ne**ho**da*	буря / негода
story	*opovee**dan**nya*	оповідання
straight	*prya**miy***	прямий
strange	***diw**niy*	дивний
stranger	*nezna**yo**mets'*	незнайомець
street	***voo**litsya*	вулиця
strike, on	*strayk*	страйк
strong	***sil'**niy*	сильний
stupid	*door**niy***	дурний
suddenly	***rap**tom*	раптом
sure/certain	*oopewneniy*	упевнений
Are you sure?	*vi wpewnenee?*	Ви впевнені?
surprise	*nespo**dee**vanka*	несподіванка
sweet	*so**lod**kiy*	солодкий
sweets/candy	*tsoo**ker**ki*	цукерки
swim (v)	***pla**vati*	плавати

T

take	***bra**ti/**wzya**ti*	брати / взяти
I'll take one.	*ya veez'**moo o**din*	Я візьму один.
Can I take this?	***mozh**na **wzya**ti tse?*	Можна взяти це?
talk	*rozmow**lya**ti*	розмовляти
tall	*vi**so**kiy*	високий
tasty	*smach**niy***	смачний
tax	*po**da**tok*	податок
telephone (n)	*tele**fon***	телефон
telephone (v)	*telefonoo**va**ti*	телефонувати
telephone book	*tele**fon**na **kni**ha*	телефонна книга
temperature	*tempera**too**ra*	температура
tent	*na**met***	намет
thank	***dya**koovati*	дякувати
Thank you.	***dya**kooyoo*	Дякую.
there	*tam*	там
thick	***hus**tiy*	густий
thief	***zlo**deey*	злодій
thin	***ton**kiy*	тонкий
think	***doo**mati*	думати
thirsty, I'm	*ya **kho**choo **pi**ti.*	Я хочу пити.
ticket	*kvi**tok***	квиток
time	*chas*	час
What time is it?	***ko**tra ho**di**na?*	Котра година?
I don't have time.	*ya ne **ma**yoo **cha**soo.*	Я не маю часу.
tin opener	*veedkri**vach**ka*	відкривачка
tip (gratuity)	*chayo**vee***	чайові
tired, I'm	*ya sto**miw**sya*	Я стомився. (m)
	*ya sto**mi**lasya*	Я стомилася. (f)

together	***ra**zom*	разом
toilet	*tooa**let***	туалет
toilet paper	*tooa**let**niy pa**peer***	туалетний папір
tonight	*s'o**hod**nee*	сьогодні
	*oo**ve**cheree*	увечері
too (also)	*ta**kozh***	також
too	*(za)**nad**to*	(за)надто
torch/flashlight	*leekh**ta**rik*	ліхтарик
touch	*tor**ka**tisya*	торкатися
tour	*eks**koor**seeya*	екскурсія
I'm touring Ukraine.	*ya podoro**zhoo**yoo po ookra**yee**nee.*	Я подорожую по Україні.
tourist	*too**rist***	турист
toward	*do*	до
town	***mees**to*	місто
track (path)	***stezh**ka*	стежка
track (railway)	***ko**leeya*	колія
transit	*tran**zi**tom*	транзитом
translate	*perekla**da**ti*	перекладати
translation	*pe**re**klad*	переклад
trekking	*po**kheed***	похід
trip	*po**yeez**dka/**po**dorozh*	поїздка / подорож
true	***veer**niy*	вірний
trust (faith)	*do**vee**ra*	довіра
try (attempt)	***spro**boovati*	спробувати
try (food)	*kooshtoo**va**ti*	куштувати
try on (clothing)	*primee**rya**ti*	приміряти

U

uncomfortable	*nezrooch**niy***	незручний
under	*peed*	під

understand	*rozoo**mee**ti*	розуміти
I don't understand.	*ya ne rozoo**mee**yoo.*	Я не розумію.
Do you understand me?	*vi rozoo**mee**yete **me**ne?*	Ви розумієте мене?
unemployed	*bezro**beet**niy*	безробітний
university	*ooneeversi**tet***	університет
unsafe	*nebez**pech**niy*	небезпечний
until	*do*	до
upstairs	*naho**ree***	нагорі
urgent	*termee**no**viy*	терміновий
useful	*ko**ris**niy/ po**treeb**niy*	корисний / потрібний
useless	*neko**ris**niy/ nepo**treeb**niy*	некорисний / непотрібний

V

vacation	*ka**nee**kooli*	канікули
vaccination	*vaktsina**tsee**ya/ **shchep**lennya*	вакцинація / щеплення
vain, in	***mar**no*	марно
valuable	*kosh**tow**niy*	коштовний
value	***var**teest'*	вартість
various	***reez**niy*	різний
very	***doo**zhe*	дуже
view	*vid*	вид
village	*se**lo***	село
visit	*veedvee**doo**vati*	відвідувати
vomit	*blyoo**va**ti*	блювати
vote	*holosoo**va**ti*	голосувати

W

wait	*che**ka**ti*	чекати
Wait a moment!	*khvi**li**nochkoo!*	Хвилиночку!
walk (n)	*pro**hoo**lyanka*	прогулянка
Do you want to go for a walk?	*vi **kho**chete pee**ti** pohoo**lya**ti?*	Ви хочете піти погуляти?
walk (v)	*hoo**lya**ti*	гуляти
want	*kho**tee**ti*	хотіти
I want ...	*ya **khochoo** ...*	Я хочу ...
We want ...	*mi **khochemo** ...*	Ми хочемо ...
Do you want ...?	*vi **khochete** ...?*	Ви хочете ...?
war	*vee**yna***	війна
warm	***tep**liy*	теплий
wash (oneself)	***mi**tisya*	митися
I have to wash.	*me**nee** **tre**ba po**mi**tisya.*	Мені треба помитися.
wash (clothes, etc)	***pra**ti*	прати
They need to be washed.	*yeekh **tre**ba **vi**prati.*	Їх треба випрати.
watch (n)	*ho**din**nik*	годинник
watch (v)	*oh**lya**dati/ spostere**eha**ti*	оглядати/ спостерігати
Watch out!	*obe**rezh**no!*	Обережно!
water	***vo**da*	вода
way	*do**ro**ha*	дорога
Which way?	*ya**ko**yoo do**ro**hoyoo?*	Якою дорогою?
wealthy	*ba**ha**tiy*	багатий
weather	*po**ho**da*	погода
Welcome!	***shchi**ro vee**ta**yoo!*	Щиро вітаю!
well (n)	*kri**ni**tsya*	криниця

wet	*mokriy*	мокрий
what	*shcho*	що
What time is it?	*kotra hodina?*	Котра година?
What did you say?	*shcho vi skazali?*	Що ви сказали?
when	*koli*	коли
where	*de*	де
who	*khto*	хто
Who do I ask?	*koho spitati?*	Кого спитати?
win	*vihrati*	виграти
wise	*moodriy*	мудрий
wish (n)	*bazhannya*	бажання
wish (v)	*bazhati*	бажати
with	*z/eez/zee*	з / із / зі
within	*wseredinee*	всередині
without	*bez*	без
work (n)	*robota*	робота
work (v)	*pratsyoovati*	працювати
world	*sveet*	світ
worse (adj)	*heershiy*	гірший
worse (adv)	*heershe*	гірше
write	*pisati*	писати
I'm writing ...	*ya pishoo*	Я пишу
She is writing ...	*vona pishe*	Вона пише
wrong	*pomilkoviy*	помилковий
You are wrong.	*vi pomilyayetesya*	Ви помиляєтеся.

Y

year	*reek*	рік
two years ago	*dva roki tomoo*	два роки тому
Yes.	*tak*	Так.

yesterday	***oochora***	учора
young	***molodiy***	молодий

Z

zone	***zona***	зона
zoo	***zo-opark***	зоопарк

Emergencies

Help!	*ryatooyte!*	Рятуйте!
	dopomozheet'!	Допоможіть!
Watch out!	*oberezhno!*	Обережно!
Go away!	*het'/eedeet'*	Геть / Ідіть
	(eedi) zveedsi!	(іди) звідси!
Get lost!	*znikni!*	Зникни!
Stop it!	*pripineet'*	Припиніть
	(pripini)!	(припини)!
Police!	*meeleetseeya!*	Міліція!
Thief!	*zlodeey!*	Злодій!
	hrabooyoot'!	Грабують!

Call a doctor!
(viklichte) leekarya! — (Викличте) лікаря!

Call an ambulance!
viklichte shvidkoo dopomohoo! — Викличте швидку допомогу!

I am ill.
ya khvoriy/khvora — Я хворий (m)/хвора (f).
menee pohano — мені погано.

I am lost.
ya zablookaw — Я заблукав. (m)
ya zablookala — Я заблукала. (f)

I've been ...	*mene ...*	Мене …
beaten up	*pobili*	побили
injured	*poranili*	поранили

raped	*ZHvaltoo**va**li*	зґвалтували
robbed	*pohraboo**va**li*	пограбували

I've lost	*ya zahoo**biw**/ zahoo**bi**la ...*	Я загубив (m)/ загубила (f) ...
my bag	***soom**koo*	сумку
my credit card	*kre**dit**noo **kart**koo*	кредитну картку
my money	***hro**shee*	гроші
my passport	***pas**port*	паспорт
my travellers' cheques	*do**rozh**nee **che**ki*	дорожні чеки

Could I use the telephone?
***mozh**na (zveed**si**/veed vas) podzvo**ni**ti?* — Можна (звідси/від вас) подзвонити?

I want to phone my embassy.
*ya **kho**choo zatelefonoo**va**ti do po**sol'**stva mo**ye**yee kra**yee**ni* — Я хочу зателефонувати до посольства моєї країни.

I have medical insurance.
*oo **me**ne me**dich**ne strakhoo**van**nya* — У мене медичне страхування.

I need a lawyer.
me**nee pot**ree**ben advo**kat — Мені потрібен адвокат.

I have no money.
*oo **me**ne ne**ma**ye hro**shey*** — У мене немає грошей.

I need help.
***me**nee pot**reeb**na dopo**mo**ha* — Мені потрібна допомога.

I want to go home!
*ya **kho**choo do**do**moo!* — Я хочу додому!

Index

LONELY PLANET PHRASEBOOKS

Complete your travel experience with a Lonely Planet phrasebook. Developed for the independent traveller, the phrasebooks enable you to communicate confidently in any practical situation – and get to know the local people and their culture.

Skipping lengthy details on where to get your drycleaning ironed, information in the phrasebooks covers bargaining, customs and protocol, how to address people and introduce yourself, explanations of local ways of telling the time, dealing with bureaucracy and bargaining, plus plenty of ways to share your interests and learn from locals.

Arabic (Egyptian)
Arabic (Moroccan)
Australian
Introduction to Australian English, Aboriginal and Torres Strait languages.
Baltic States
Covers Estonian, Latvian and Lithuanian.
Bengali
Brazilian
Burmese
Cantonese
Central Europe
Covers Czech, French, German, Hungarian, Italian and Slovak.
Eastern Europe
Covers Bulgarian, Czech, Hungarian, Polish, Romanian and Slovak.
Ethiopian (Amharic)
Fijian
Greek
Hindi/Urdu
Indonesian
Japanese
Korean
Lao
Latin American (Spanish)
Mandarin
Mediterranean Europe
Covers Albanian, Greek, Italian, Macedonian, Maltese, Serbian & Croatian and Slovene.
Mongolian
Nepali
Papua New Guinea (Pidgin)
Pilipino
Quechua
Russian
Scandinavian Europe
Covers Danish, Finnish, Icelandic, Norwegian and Swedish.
Sri Lanka
Swahili
Thai
Thai Hill Tribes
Tibetan
Turkish
Ukranian
USA
Introduction to US English, Vernacular Talk, Native American languages and Hawaiian.
Vietnamese
Western Europe
Useful words and phrases in Basque, Catalan, Dutch, French, German, Irish, Portuguese and Spanish (Castilian).

LONELY PLANET AUDIO PACKS

Audio packs are an innovative combination of a cassette/CD and phrasebook presented in an attractive cloth wallet made from indigenous textiles by local communities.

The cassette/CD presents each language in an interactive format. A number of successful language teaching techniques are used, enabling listeners to remember useful words and phrases with little effort and in an enjoyable way.

Travellers will learn essential words and phrases – and their correct pronunciation – by participating in a realistic story. The scripts have been developed in the belief that the best way to learn a new language is to hear it, then to practise it in the context in which you will use it. The emphasis is on effective communication.

The cassette/CD complements the relevant phrasebook, and the cloth wallet makes the pack an attractive and convenient package – easy to display in shops and useful and practical for travellers.

Cassettes & CDs

- complement phrasebooks
- realistic storylines explore situations that will be useful for all travellers
- languages are spoken by native speakers
- listeners learn key words and phrases in repetition exercises, then hear them used in context
- realistic sound effects and indigenous music used throughout
- length: 80 minutes

Cloth Pack

- ticket-wallet size – suitable for airline tickets, notes etc
- made from traditional textiles woven and sewn by local communities
- cardboard reinforced and sealed in plastic for easy display
- size: 140 x 260 mm

Available now: Indonesian audio pack; Japanese audio pack; Thai audio pack

PLANET TALK

Lonely Planet's FREE quarterly newsletter

Every issue is packed with up-to-date travel news and advice including:

- a letter from Lonely Planet co-founders Tony and Maureen Wheeler
- go behind the scenes on the road with a Lonely Planet author
- feature article on an important and topical travel issue
- a selection of recent letters from travellers
- details on forthcoming Lonely planet promotions
- complete list of Lonely Planet products

To join our mailing list contact any Lonely Planet office.

LONELY PLANET PUBLICATIONS

AUSTRALIA
PO Box 617, Hawthorn 3122, Victoria
tel: (03) 9819 1877 fax: (03) 9819 6459
e-mail: talk2us@lonelyplanet.com.au

USA
Embarcadero West,
155 Filbert St, Suite 251,
Oakland, CA 94607
tel: (510) 893 8555
TOLL FREE: 800 275-8555
fax: (510) 893 8563
e-mail: info@lonelyplanet.com

UK
10 Barley Mow Passage, Chiswick,
London W4 4PH
tel: (0181) 742 3161 fax: (0181) 742 2772
e-mail: 100413.3551@compuserve.com

FRANCE:
71 bis rue du Cardinal Lemoine, 75005
Paris
tel: 1 44 32 06 20 fax: 1 46 34 72 55
e-mail: 100560.415@compuserve.com

World Wide Web: http://www.lonelyplanet.com